Privacy Risk Analysis of Online Social Networks

Synthesis Lectures on Information Security, Privacy, and Trust

Editors
Elisa Bertino, *Purdue University*
Elena Ferrari, *University of Insubria, Italy*

Founding Editor
Ravi Sandhu, *University of Texas, San Antonio*

The series publishes short books on topics pertaining to all aspects of the theory and practice of Information Security, Privacy, and Trust. In addition to the research topics, the series also solicits lectures on legal, policy, social, business, and economic issues addressed to a technical audience of scientists and engineers. Lectures on significant industry developments by leading practitioners are also solicited.

Privacy Risk Analysis of Online Social Networks
Sourya Joyee De and Abdessamad Imine
2020

Anomaly Detection as a Service: Challenges, Advances, and Opportunities
Danfeng (Daphne) Yao, Xiaokui Shu, Long Cheng, and Salvatore J. Stolfo
2017

Cyber-Physical Security and Privacy in the Electric Smart Grid
Bruce McMillin and Thomas Roth
2017

Blocks and Chains: Introduction to Bitcoin, Cryptocurrencies, and Their Consensus Mechanisms
Aljosha Judmayer, Nicholas Stifter, Katharina Krombholz, and Edgar Weippl
2017

Digital Forensic Science: Issues, Methods, and Challenges
Vassil Roussev
2016

Differential Privacy: From Theory to Practice
Ninghui Li, Min Lyu, Dong Su, and Weining Yang
2016

Privacy Risk Analysis
Sourya Joyee De and Daniel Le Métayer
2016

Introduction to Secure Outsourcing Computation
Xiaofeng Chen
2016

Database Anonymization: Privacy Models, Data Utility, and Microaggregation-based
Inter-model Connections
Josep Domingo-Ferrer, David Sánchez, and Jordi Soria-Comas
2016

Automated Software Diversity
Per Larsen, Stefan Brunthaler, Lucas Davi, Ahmad-Reza Sadeghi, and Michael Franz
2015

Trust in Social Media
Jiliang Tang and Huan Liu
2015

Physically Unclonable Functions (PUFs): Applications, Models, and Future Directions
Christian Wachsmann and Ahmad-Reza Sadeghi
2014

Usable Security: History, Themes, and Challenges
Simson Garfinkel and Heather Richter Lipford
2014

Reversible Digital Watermarking: Theory and Practices
Ruchira Naskar and Rajat Subhra Chakraborty
2014

Mobile Platform Security
N. Asokan, Lucas Davi, Alexandra Dmitrienko, Stephan Heuser, Kari Kostiainen, Elena
Reshetova, and Ahmad-Reza Sadeghi
2013

Security and Trust in Online Social Networks
Barbara Carminati, Elena Ferrari, and Marco Viviani
2013

RFID Security and Privacy
Yingjiu Li, Robert H. Deng, and Elisa Bertino
2013

Hardware Malware
Christian Krieg, Adrian Dabrowski, Heidelinde Hobel, Katharina Krombholz, and Edgar Weippl
2013

Private Information Retrieval
Xun Yi, Russell Paulet, and Elisa Bertino
2013

Privacy for Location-based Services
Gabriel Ghinita
2013

Enhancing Information Security and Privacy by Combining Biometrics with Cryptography
Sanjay G. Kanade, Dijana Petrovska-Delacrétaz, and Bernadette Dorizzi
2012

Analysis Techniques for Information Security
Anupam Datta, Somesh Jha, Ninghui Li, David Melski, and Thomas Reps
2010

Operating System Security
Trent Jaeger
2008

Privacy Risk Analysis of Online Social Networks

Sourya Joyee De and Abdessamad Imine

ISBN: 978-3-031-01227-3   paperback
ISBN: 978-3-031-02355-2   ebook
ISBN: 978-3-031-03483-1   hardcover

DOI 10.1007/978-3-031-02355-2

A Publication in the Springer series
SYNTHESIS LECTURES ON INFORMATION SECURITY, PRIVACY, AND TRUST

Lecture #23
Series Editors: Elisa Bertino, *Purdue University*
                Elena Ferrari, *University of Insubria, Italy*
Founding Editor: Ravi Sandhu, *University of Texas, San Antonio*
Series ISSN
Print 1945-9742   Electronic 1945-9750

Privacy Risk Analysis of Online Social Networks

Sourya Joyee De
Indian Institute of Management Raipur, India

Abdessamad Imine
Lorraine University, LORIA-CNRS-INRIA Nancy Grand-Est, France

SYNTHESIS LECTURES ON INFORMATION SECURITY, PRIVACY, AND TRUST #23

ABSTRACT

The social benefit derived from Online Social Networks (OSNs) can lure users to reveal un-precedented volumes of personal data to an online audience that is much less trustworthy than their offline social circle. Even if a user hides his personal data from some users and shares with others, privacy settings of OSNs may be bypassed, thus leading to various privacy harms such as identity theft, stalking, or discrimination. Therefore, users need to be assisted in understanding the privacy risks of their OSN profiles as well as managing their privacy settings so as to keep such risks in check, while still deriving the benefits of social network participation.

This book presents to its readers how privacy risk analysis concepts such as privacy harms and risk sources can be used to develop mechanisms for privacy scoring of user profiles and for supporting users in privacy settings management in the context of OSNs. Privacy scoring helps detect and minimize the risks due to the dissemination and use of personal data. The book also discusses many open problems in this area to encourage further research.

KEYWORDS

privacy, online social networks, privacy risk, privacy risk analysis, privacy harms, social benefits, privacy management, privacy settings

Contents

Acknowledgments . . . . **xiii**

1 Introduction 1
    1.1 Chapter Overview 3

2 Terminology and Definitions 5
    2.1 Attributes 5
        2.1.1 Privacy Settings of Attributes 7
    2.2 Risk Sources 8
    2.3 Data Inference 10
    2.4 Threat 11
    2.5 Privacy Harm 12
    2.6 Privacy Risks 14
    2.7 Privacy Risk Analysis 14

3 Dimensions of Privacy Scoring in OSNs 17
    3.1 Type of Data 17
    3.2 Assumptions About the User 19
    3.3 Privacy Settings 19
    3.4 Risk Sources 19
    3.5 Privacy Metrics 20
        3.5.1 Sensitivity 20
        3.5.2 Visibility 21
        3.5.3 Reachability 21
    3.6 Data Inference 22
    3.7 Suggestion of Countermeasures 22

4 Attribute Visibility in OSN 23
    4.1 Visibility Matrix 23
    4.2 Construction of Visibility Matrix 24
    4.3 An Illustration 29
    4.4 Open Problems 30

5 Harm Trees for OSNs **31**

   5.1   Harm Trees 31

   5.2   Construction of Harm trees 32

       5.2.1   Harm Likelihood 32

   5.3   Harm Expressions 34

   5.4   Harm Database 34

   5.5   Open Problems 35

6 Privacy Risk Analysis in OSNs **37**

   6.1   An Overview 37

   6.2   PrivOSN in Details 39

       6.2.1   Computation of Accuracy 41

       6.2.2   Evaluation of Harm Likelihoods 42

       6.2.3   Computation Profile Similarity 43

       6.2.4   Presentation of Privacy Risk to the User 44

   6.3   Residual Risks 45

   6.4   Open Problems 45

7 Social Benefits **49**

   7.1   Social Ties 49

   7.2   Social Capital 50

   7.3   Understanding Social Benefits 51

       7.3.1   Social Benefit Criteria 51

       7.3.2   Attributes and Social Benefit Criteria 54

   7.4   Evaluation of Social Benefit 55

   7.5   Open Problems 56

8 Choosing the Right Privacy Settings **59**

   8.1   Privacy and Social Benefit Tradeoff in Privacy Management 60

   8.2   An Integer Programming Model 62

       8.2.1   Balancing Privacy Risks and Social Benefits 62

   8.3   Formulation of the IP Problem 64

       8.3.1   Objective Function 64

       8.3.2   Privacy Risk Constraints 64

       8.3.3   Social Benefit Constraints 65

       8.3.4   Privacy Setting Constraints 66

   8.4   Open Problems 66

9   **Conclusion** **69**

A   **Notations and Their Meanings** **71**

B   **Comparison of Privacy Scoring Mechanisms** **73**

C   **Cases 3 and 4** **75**

Bibliography **79**

Authors' Biographies **95**

Acknowledgments

The first author acknowledges the resources and support provided by the Indian Institute of Management Raipur without which the completion of the manuscript would not have been possible.

The authors also acknowledge the support of Lorraine University, LORIA-CNRS-INRIA Nancy Grand-Est, French ANR Project SEQUOIA, Cisco San Jose, CA, USA, and the Grand-Est Region.

Sourya Joyee De and Abdessamad Imine
October 2020

CHAPTER 1

Introduction

According to a recent survey by Pew Research Center [65], about seven out of ten Americans use Facebook. There are about 280 million Facebook users in India alone [134]. Among French Internet users, this social network giant has a penetration rate of about 76% [133]. Taking into account other online social networks (OSNs) like Twitter and LinkedIn, the worldwide figures of OSN usage would be enormous.

What is it that makes OSNs so attractive? Users derive many benefits from participating in OSNs. Social networks allow their users to stay in touch with family and friends and to connect with others having similar interests and hobbies [88, 126].

When users open an account on an OSN, their first task is to populate their profile with various information so as to introduce themselves and establish a basis of forming connections with other members. While doing so, users reveal a lot of personal data about themselves, ranging from their age and gender to more intimate details like their interests to their friends, their friends-of-friends, as well as strangers.

Even when users hide these data, inferring these data is often not very difficult given what the friends of the users reveal [7, 99, 161]. The simple social network of Ana and her friends in Figure 1.1 is a useful illustration. Ana does not reveal her age to anyone, but most of her friends reveal their ages to their friends, friends-of-friends, and even strangers. Since Ana's friends are likely to be close to her own age, by the property of homophily [97], it is possible for another user to guess her age.

OSN members who are the audience of the personal data revealed by users may include future employers, colleagues, relatives, and even complete strangers. These actors may misuse the personal data to cause various privacy harms such as identity theft, discrimination, or sexual predation, for the user. For example, a future employer may assess the user's OSN profile to understand his suitability for a job and decide not to make him the offer when they find that the user has a certain political orientation or religious belief.

Major OSN providers enable users to choose the audience to whom their personal data should be visible. An OSN may allow users to choose the privacy settings of their data such that it is kept private or revealed to friends, friends-of-friends, or the public. Some OSNs also offer the possibility of drawing up a customized list of audiences for different publications such as attributes, posts, and comments. When faced with such options, users may not fully comprehend the privacy implications of their choices, given their limited expertise.

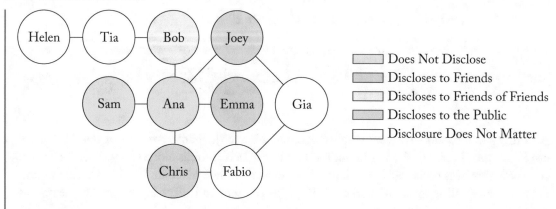

Figure 1.1: The target user, Ana, her friends, and the revelation of Ana's age.

Only when users clearly understand the risks and benefits of their current privacy settings can they be motivated to switch to more privacy-protective ones. This view is now being promoted by the new European Union General Data Protection Regulation (EU GDPR) [56] (Recitals 7 and 39) by emphasizing on the data subjects' control over their personal data and that they should be made aware of the risks related to personal data processing.

While users generally have a more or less precise idea of the benefits of OSN use, privacy risks are more difficult for them to assess. Further, once they understand the risks they face, they need some form of guidance to choose the *right* privacy settings as the decision-making process is incredibly complex. Users have little idea how different combinations of personal data can be exploited by different types of audiences to lead to privacy risks. At the same time, while pursuing privacy protection, the choice of privacy settings should not be so restrictive that they lose the benefits for which they participate in an OSN.

The EU GDPR has made it mandatory for data controllers to carry out data protection impact assessment (DPIA) for certain types of personal data processing activities. Researchers have also focused on the development of methodologies for privacy impact assessment (PIA) and privacy risk analysis (PRA), the technical core of PIA, to aid data controllers in understanding the privacy risks of their data processing activities. The use of privacy risk analysis concepts for helping users in their privacy related decision-making processes is relatively new [39–41, 46]. OSNs constitute an interesting application area in this context, not only due to the fact that they present significant privacy risks for users, but also because users can truly derive the benefits from using these platforms only if they reveal personal data.

This book presents to its readers the intersection of online social networks and the utilization of privacy risk analysis concepts from the viewpoint of users. It delineates ways in which users can be supported to protect themselves from privacy harms arising from OSNs. More precisely, it gives an overview of privacy scoring that makes users aware of the level of privacy risks of their OSN profiles and privacy management support for users for their OSN profiles, based on privacy risk analysis concepts. The idea is to introduce readers to the works that initiated this area and to encourage further research in this direction. The book is primarily written keeping in mind an audience consisting of researchers, students, computer scientists, and legal scholars interested in privacy, privacy risk analysis, and social networks,

Many of the examples used in the book are inspired from Facebook, one of the most popular OSNs to date. However, the discussions can be easily extrapolated to other OSNs. Also, the EU GDPR has been referred to multiple times for its risk-based approach to data protection. In fact, it is one of the most comprehensive data protection regulations in force and has encouraged research into several directions of privacy protection, especially privacy risk analysis.

1.1   CHAPTER OVERVIEW

Below, we present a brief overview of the chapters that follow.

Chapter 2 introduces the reader to the terminology and notations used in the rest of the book. In this chapter, special attention has been paid to familiarize users with the concepts of privacy risk and privacy risk analysis and related notions such as privacy harms, risk sources, and threats.

Chapter 3 puts forth the different dimensions of privacy scoring methods in OSNs such as the type of data these methods take into account, their assumptions about the user, various privacy metrics such as visibility and sensitivity of data that influence privacy scores, the types of countermeasures proposed based on privacy scores, and so on. These dimensions set apart one privacy scoring method from the other and therefore tell the reader the unique features of different methods.

Chapter 4 describes how the visibility of attributes revealed in a user profile can be determined. As discussed in Chapter 3, visibility is an important privacy metric that affects the privacy scores of users.

Chapter 5 introduces the reader to the concept of harm trees in the context of OSNs, in details. Harm trees link the exploitation of attributes revealed by user profiles by various risk sources to threats and ultimately to privacy harms. The chapter also describes how harm trees can be constructed and how harm expressions can be derived from harm trees and evaluated.

Chapter 6 discusses a privacy scoring method for OSNs based on privacy risk analysis. This method utilizes the computation of visibility and uses the notion of harm trees described in Chapters 4 and 5, respectively. The chapter offers the readers an insight into the meaning of the privacy score, thus derived, for the user and, finally, points out to some open problems related to PRA-based privacy scoring.

Chapter 7 turns the readers' attention to the social benefits that users can derive from their participation in OSNs, especially by revealing attributes in their profiles. Four major benefits and how they are linked to the revelation of different sets of personal data are described. Finally, the chapter also discusses a method to evaluate the overall social benefit derived from an OSN profile.

Chapter 8 directs the reader to the countermeasure of privacy management by the user through the appropriate choice of privacy settings of the personal data revealed in their profile, while at the same time taking into account the social benefits derived from the profile. The chapter provides a brief overview of different types of works in privacy management that have taken into account this trade-off and then discusses in detail a method, based on privacy risk analysis, that helps users choose the right privacy settings. The chapter ends with some open problems in PRA-based privacy settings management.

Finally, we leave our concluding thoughts in Chapter 9.

CHAPTER 2

Terminology and Definitions

Users may publish various personal data in their OSN profiles, such as their birthday, gender, interests, education, and workplace, in the form of *attributes*. They can choose appropriate *privacy settings*, provided by the OSN, to reveal the attributes to suitable audiences such as friends, friends-of-friends, and even strangers who are members of the OSN. These audiences may become *risk sources* leading to a variety of *threats* such as unintended access to user *attributes*. These threats ultimately cause *privacy harms*, such as identity theft, for the user.

These concepts form the basis of the discussions in this book. This chapter formally defines them and provides appropriate examples. The chapter also briefly introduces the concepts of *data inference*, *privacy risks*, and *privacy risk analysis* that are important for the current discourse. A list of notations frequently used in the book can be found in Appendix A.

In the rest of the book, the *target user T* or simply the *user* represents the OSN user whose privacy is of our primary concern. A privacy expert is a person or a team who has sufficient expertise in the domain of privacy, especially in the context of OSNs, such as a data protection authority like the CNIL[1] in France, a privacy research group, and so on.

The use of the terms privacy harms, threats, and risk sources and their relationship with attributes have been inspired from previous research [39, 43, 68, 75, 79, 108, 149]. The examples of attributes, privacy settings, and risk sources used in the discourse have been inspired from those in Facebook.

The book focuses on examples from Facebook due to a number of reasons [38]. First, Facebook is one of the most popular OSNs [65, 134]. Second, it has been questioned over the years by regulators and privacy advocates about its privacy invasive practices [92] and investigated by various data protection authorities. Researchers [11, 39, 68, 75, 77, 79, 85, 108, 122, 129, 145, 146, 149] have uncovered various privacy harms that can result from the personal data disclosed in this platform. Facebook has also recently suffered various security and privacy breaches including the Cambridge Analytica scandal [92], the breach of up to 50 million user accounts due to bugs in its "View as" functionality [91], and the disclosure of user data to Microsoft's Bing search engine and Amazon [14, 36].

2.1 ATTRIBUTES

A user profile in an OSN consists of

---

[1]Commission nationale de l'informatique et des libertés.

  - a *static* part, not updated very frequently and more or less of constant size and

  - a *dynamic* part, which is updated frequently and of varying size.

In the static part of the profile, a user describes himself in terms of his personal data, referred to as *attributes*, such as his gender, age, and interests. In the dynamic part of the profile, the user frequently reveals personal data through posts, likes and comments.

The *attributes* of the user provide a first impression about him to other OSN users. They constitute the basis of building new friendships as well as reviving and enhancing existing ones. The book focuses on the privacy of these attributes.[2]

Generally speaking, the term *personal data* can encompass a wide variety of data. This is evident from the interpretation of personal data in the EU GDPR [56] which uses this term to mean

"information relating to an identified or identifiable natural person."[3]

In the context of this book, the set of all personal data (as defined by the GDPR) is the universal set. The universal set thus contains all data that qualify as personal data according to the definition put forth in the GDPR. The set of attributes ($\mathbb{A}_D$) is its subset. The elements in $\mathbb{A}_D$ depend on the OSN under consideration.

While popular social networks like Facebook and LinkedIn may use some common attributes such as age, gender, and workplace, each of them also uses attributes specific to the purpose of their usage. For example, relationship status is an attribute in Facebook, but not in LinkedIn. So, for different OSNs, the elements of the attribute set $\mathbb{A}_D$ would be different.

For simplicity, we assume that $\mathbb{A}_D$ also includes personal data that are simple concatenations of attributes. For example, date of birth (e.g., April 18, 1983) is a concatenation of birthday (e.g., April 18th) and birth year (e.g., 1983).

Below, we formally define attributes.

Definition 2.1   An **attribute** is a personal data[4] item considered to be a part of the user profile information in an OSN. It helps to introduce a user to other users of the same OSN.

In an OSN, each user has the set $\mathbb{A}_D$ of attributes as specified in Table 2.1.[5] Other attributes may also be used in different OSNs, but this discourse only considers the set in Table 2.1.

Each attribute $d \in \mathbb{A}_D$ may assume different values for different users. The ith value of d is d_{v_i}. To illustrate, the attribute gender (Gen) may assume the values *male* for user T_1 and

---

[2]Consideration of the dynamic part is another complex problem, and deserves separate attention.

[3]The GDPR defines *"an identifiable natural person is one who can be identified, directly or indirectly, in particular by reference to an identifier such as a name, an identification number, location data, an online identifier or to one or more factors specific to the physical, physiological, genetic, mental, economic, cultural or social identity of that natural person."*

[4]This book follows the definition of personal data as in the European Union's General Data Protection Regulation (EU GDPR) [56].

[5]The attributes presented in this table are inspired from the popular OSN Facebook.

Table 2.1: The set of attributes ($\mathbb{A}_D$), codes representing these attributes, and examples of attribute values (d_{v_i})

Code	Attributes (d)	Examples of Values (d_{v_i})
B.Yr	Birth year	1990, 1984, …
B.Dt	Birthday	April 20, December 19, …
Gen	Gender	Male, Female, …
Ph	Phone number	66775864, 65879001, …
G.Int	Gender interests	Women, men, both, …
H.Add	Home address	20 Mayfair Street, Kolkata 700004, 54 Rue de Bruxelles, Nancy 54000, …
W.Pl	Workplace	Inria Nancy Grand-Est, IIM Calcutta, …
W.desig	Work Designation	Researcher, General Manager, …
Edu	Education level	Ph.D., M.Sc., …
Pol	Political views	Left, Center, …
Rel	Religious views	Hinduism, Atheism, …
RStat	Relationship status	Single, Married, …
Int	Interests	Swimming, Cricket, Art, Music, …

female for user T_2. So, the set of values corresponding to the attribute Gen may be given as {*male,female,others*}. The attribute birth year (B.Yr) may assume a valid representation of a year, for example, 1994. Table 2.1 presents some illustrative valid values for the attributes in $\mathbb{A}_D$.

The current discussion assumes that providing a name or a pseudonym is mandatory and can be seen by everyone on the OSN. So, a name or a pseudonym is not considered an attribute.

2.1.1 PRIVACY SETTINGS OF ATTRIBUTES

The visibility of attributes to other users can be limited by users by choosing the appropriate *privacy settings*. Users can select from a range of privacy settings to ensure that attribute values are visible only to their desirable audiences in the OSN.

The privacy settings[6] considered in this book are:

---

[6]These privacy settings are inspired by those traditionally made available by Facebook. Recently, however, there have been modifications in the privacy settings that Facebook offers. Specifically, the friends-of-friends option has been removed and

1. *"private"*: makes an attribute value visible to no one;

2. *"friends"*: makes an attribute value visible to only friends;

3. *"friends-of-friends"*: makes an attribute value visible to friends and friends-of-friends; and

4. *"public"*: makes an attribute value visible to all users of the OSN.

Due to the privacy settings, from the overall user profile, the true values of only some attributes, i.e., the ones disclosed by the user, can be viewed by other OSN members. This constitutes only a partial view of the user's *real profile*. All attributes disclosed by the user himself to a certain group of OSN members (for example, his friends) are known to them with full confidence.

To obtain a complete view of the user's profile, the values of undisclosed attributes must be inferred, correctly or incorrectly, by these OSN members. They can used different types of inference methods for this purpose, but are never fully confident about the inferred attribute value. Therefore, the inferred attributes and the disclosed attributes together lead to a *virtual* view of the user. In general, this view is only partially correct.

The *vicinity* of the user consists of the friends of the user in the OSN. The user's value for an attribute may be inferred by risk sources based on the values of the same or related attribute(s) disclosed by the user's vicinity.

2.2 RISK SOURCES

A first step to protect user privacy in OSNs is to understand the risk sources, i.e., entities whose actions may lead to privacy breaches. In the security literature, these entities are often referred to as *adversary* or *attacker*. The terminology *risk source* has already been used in the context of privacy risk analysis of personal data processing systems. We adapt the definition of risk sources from this literature [43, 45, 47] for an OSN.

Definition 2.2 A **risk source** is any entity (individual or organization) that may process (legally or illegally) data belonging to the target user and whose actions may directly or indirectly, intentionally or unintentionally, lead to privacy harms.

In the context of attribute inference attacks in OSNs, attackers may be any party who has interests in user attributes, such as cyber criminals, OSN provider, advertiser, data broker, and surveillance agencies [62, 63]. The OSN provider and malicious advertisers can exploit the user's personal data leading to various privacy breaches such as micro-targeting and discrimination [11, 11, 37, 77, 122, 129, 145, 146].

---

attributes or posts can also be shared with some specific friends or all friends except some specific ones. The discourse can be adapted to these changes and also to the privacy settings offered by other OSNs.

This book focuses on privacy risks due to OSN members (apart from the user himself).[7] Therefore, risk sources include:

1. the friends of the user ($A.1$, denoting risk sources at level 1 with respect to the user);

2. the friends-of-friends of the user ($A.2$, denoting risk sources at level 2 with respect to the user); and

3. the strangers to the user ($A.3$, denoting all risk sources beyond the friends-of-friends of the user, i.e., at level 3 and beyond with respect to the user).

These risk sources, who are members of the OSN, can assume different roles with respect to the user, such as a potential employer, a colleague, a relative or a neighbor, a stalker, and even an advertiser. Whereas a colleague or a relative is likely to be a friend of the user ($A.1$), a stalker or an advertiser is more likely to be a stranger ($A.3$).

These risk sources process data already made visible to them by the user or inferred by them, with motivations arising from their roles, leading to various harms. For example, a prospective employer may form a negative impression about the user based on his political views or interests. The colleagues of the user who are his friends in the OSN ($A.1$) may form a negative impression about him based on his political and/or religious views or based on his interests, sexual orientation, etc., which may negatively affect him at his workplace.

Each privacy setting implies that the attribute is visible or not visible to one or more types of risk sources. Thus, each attribute in set $\mathbb{A}_D$ can be revealed by the user to different sets of entities, i.e., friends ($A.1$), friends-of-friends ($A.2$), and strangers ($A.3$). For each attribute $d \in \mathbb{A}_D$, these levels of revelation are represented by the set $L_d = \{A.1, A.2, A.3\}$. If an attribute is revealed to $A.3$, it is also revealed to $A.2$ and $A.1$ and if an attribute is revealed to $A.2$, it is also revealed to $A.1$. An attribute which has not been revealed at any of the levels specified in L_d has been kept private.

A decision portfolio is then represented by the vector $\mathbf{x} = (x_{d,l})$ in $X = \times_{d \in \mathbb{A}_D, l \in L_d} \{0, 1\}$, where $x_{d,l} \in \{0, 1\}$ is the decision (made by the user) whether the attribute d is to be revealed ($x_{d,l} = 1$) or not ($x_{d,l} = 0$) at level l.

For example, the privacy setting of the user attribute phone number (Ph.), depending on the values of the corresponding decision variables $x_{Ph.,A.1}$, $x_{Ph.,A.2}$ and $x_{Ph.,A.3}$ is:

1. *"private"* if $x_{Ph.,A.1} = x_{Ph.,A.2} = x_{Ph.,A.3} = 0$;

2. *"friends"* if $x_{Ph.,A.1} = 1$, $x_{Ph.,A.2} = x_{Ph.,A.3} = 0$;

3. *"friends-of-friends"* if $x_{Ph.,A.1} = x_{Ph.,A.2} = 1$, $x_{Ph.,A.3} = 0$; and

4. *"public"* if $x_{Ph.,A.1} = x_{Ph.,A.2} = x_{Ph.,A.3} = 1$.

---

[7]The OSN provider has access to all personal data that the user discloses to the OSN, regardless of its privacy settings. The privacy settings are only meant to control the visibility of the data from other members of the OSN, but not the OSN provider. Nevertheless, the discourse in this book can be adapted to consider the OSN provider as a risk source. The user then needs to decide whether he wants to reveal his personal data to the OSN or not.

2.3   DATA INFERENCE

Depending on the privacy setting chosen by the user, risk sources can either see the value of an attribute published by the user or they must infer its value when it is undisclosed. When the user himself reveals an attribute to a risk source, there is no need for inferring that attribute.

For example, if the user makes his birth year (B.Yr) visible only to his friends, then the risk sources who are his friends of friends (*A*.2) cannot see his birth year and have to infer it. On the other hand, risk sources amongst his friends (*A*.1) can see this birth year without any need for inference. Since inference usually involves some inaccuracies, in this example, *A*.1 knows the value of birth year with full confidence, whereas *A*.2 knows it only with partial confidence, the level of which depends on the accuracy of the inference method used.

The values of attributes in the set $\mathbb{A}_D$ for the user can be inferred from those of attributes in $\mathbb{A}_D$ as revealed by the user's vicinity. For example, the user's age can be inferred from the age of his friends. The value of a certain user attribute can also be inferred from other attribute values the user himself reveals. For example, the user's age can be inferred from the type of music he is interested in. In a more general sense, if the risk source has access to the user's online activities such as, data revealed in other OSNs or during visit to other websites, then other personal data can be used to aid in the inference of an attribute in $\mathbb{A}_D$.

Various inference methods [10, 27, 50, 62–64, 72, 78, 118, 161] may be used by the risk source. A simple inference method would be to use the most popular value of an attribute in the target user's vicinity as the inferred value of the attribute for the target user. This method is based on the principle of homophily [97]. For example, the gender (Gen) of the target user is *female*, if most of the friends reveal their genders to be female [39].

Most existing attribute inference methods that could be used by risk sources can be classified into the following three categories. Many of these methods are based on machine learning techniques.

1. **Friend-based inference.** [50, 64, 72, 89, 99, 140, 161] This category of inference methods, relying on the intuition "*you are who you know,*" infer user attributes depending on publicly available attributes of the user's friends or other users of the OSN and the social structure among them. The basis of this type of inference methods is the *principle of homophily*, that is, two users who are socially linked share similar attributes [97]. For example, if most of the user's friends are Computer Science graduates, then it is highly likely that the user himself is also a Computer Science graduate [62, 63].

2. **Behavior-based inference.** [27, 86, 151] This category of inference methods rely on the intuition "*you are how you behave.*" They infer user atributes based on the public attributes of other users who are similar in behavior to the target user. For example, if the target user likes books, music, etc. similar to other users originally from China, then the target user is also likely from China [62, 63]. Similarly, if the target user is interested in songs by Justin

Table 2.2: Examples of attribute inferences

Inferred Attribute	Source Data	Vicinity Used
Birth year	Birth year, high school graduating year, friends' high school graduating classes [51]	Friends, friends-of-friends, regular users
Gender	Alt-texts describing contents of pictures and comments [11], Alt-texts describing contents of pictures and emojis/emoticons [119]	Friends, friends-of-friends, regular users
Gender	Movie ratings [152], first name or full name [8, 97, 99, 101, 139]	×
Race/Ethnicity	Last name [99]	×

Bieber, then the target user is likely to be a female teenager as many OSN users who are female teenagers like Justin Bieber songs [27].

3. **Friend- and behavior-based inference.** [62, 78] Friend-based inference and behavior-based inference suffer primarily from two main limitations: (1) when the aim is to infer the target user's attribute using a training dataset, these methods only take into account labeled users having the attribute, and leave out users who do not possess the attribute; and (2) they infer the attributes of the target user one by one [78]. These limitations can be overcome by using simultaneously both the social structure and the user behavior to infer user attributes.

Table 2.2 presents the different data sources from which attributes like gender, birth year, and race/ethnicity can be inferred.

2.4   THREAT

A threat refers to an event in the OSN that can lead to a privacy harm and results from the exploitation of attributes by risk sources. The notion is akin to that of feared events in [43–45]. An unintended audience such as a potential employer getting access to attributes such as religious beliefs or political affinity of a job candidate is an example of a threat.

We adapt the definition of threat from [39, 40, 42]

Definition 2.3   A **threat** is an action of a risk source or an event, with respect to one or more user attributes or the personal data derived from these attributes, resulting in a privacy harm.

There could be many types of threats in OSNs. The ones considered in this book are:

1. access to data by unintended audiences either directly due to the attributes revealed by the user or through inference of undisclosed attributes (FE.1) (for example, stalkers come to know about the target user's home address, strangers infer the gender of the target user from the genders of his friends); and

2. undesirable reactions to personal data by risk sources (FE.2) (for example, colleagues respond negatively to the user's political views) [39, 75, 108, 149].

This book takes into account only those threats that result from inappropriate privacy settings used by the target user and his friends for their attributes. It ignores threats originating from the service provider's design and/or implementation choices (such as the lack of anonymization and poor protection of data stores) due to its focus on the analysis of the OSN user profile and not the entire system.

2.5   PRIVACY HARM

The ultimate goal of privacy scoring methods for OSNs is to make users aware of the risk of privacy harms that result from the attributes revealed to different potential risk sources. Similarly, the purpose of supporting users with privacy settings management is to protect them from privacy harms while they enjoy the benefits of participating in an OSN.

The legal literature related to privacy and data protection [24, 25, 31, 35, 106, 107, 128] as well as research on privacy risk analysis [43–45, 47] have extensively discussed the concept of privacy harms. The notion has also been used in the context of OSNs [39–41].

The characterization of privacy harms is not an easy task [45]. What is considered as a privacy harm today may not be considered so in the future [107] and what is considered as privacy harm in one society or culture or country may not be so in another [45].

In general, privacy harms could be of various types [45]:

- physical harms,

- economic or financial harms,

- mental or psychological harms,

- harm to dignity or reputation, and

- societal harms.

Of these, a few such as physical harms, financial harms, and psychological harms are more relevant in the context of data revealed in OSN profiles and OSN members as risk sources. For instance, the visibility of one's sexual orientation or religious beliefs by a potential employer who is a member of the OSN leading to discrimination against a user who is seeking a job, may

Table 2.3: Examples of privacy harms

Code	Privacy Harms
h_1	Stalkers use the target user's profile to assess him as a potential victim [104]
h_2	Job screening, where a potential employer assesses the target user's profile to evaluate his suitability for a job [80]
h_3	Identity fraud/theft [58, 69]
h_4	Social isolation (including gossips, negative effect on professional life) due to personal beliefs or life choices [76, 150]
h_5	Sexual predators use the target user's profile to identify him as a potential victim
h_6	Unwanted contact where a user receives spam mails or fraudulent calls because of risk sources' access to his contact details

cause enormous psychological distress for the victim. Similarly, the access to location data such as home address may lead to economic or physical injury (e.g., burglary or murder) [45].

This book adapts the definition of privacy harm for an OSN user from the ones used in [39, 43].

Definition 2.4   A **privacy harm** is the negative impact of the use of an OSN on target user due to one or more privacy breaches.

Over the years, many types of privacy harms have been observed in real life as well as found to be possible by different research works [68, 75, 79, 103, 108, 149] from the data revealed from OSNs. Some of these harms, involving a subset of the attributes (in Table 2.1), are presented in Table 2.3.

Based on the personal data disclosed in OSN profiles, thieves or sexual predators can track, monitor, locate, and identify a user as a potential victim [159] and users can become victims of identity theft [68].

In the professional context, personal data made visible to professional contacts on OSNs may alter their favorable perceptions about the user [123], lead to biased interview call-backs in some cases [3], be used to assess a candidate's suitability for a job by an employer or for an application for admission to a university [159] and affect hiring decisions [79, 108]. Research shows that OSN profiles can also significantly affect others' impression of the user [108].

OSN users often regret sharing information on alcohol and drug use, sex, religious and political opinions, personal and family issues, work, etc., chiefly due to undesirable reactions from other users and unintended audience [149]. Users with a large number of friends and family members on their OSN friendlist are also often concerned about these OSN friends turning into "Big Brothers" controlling them through social surveillance [21].

2.6   PRIVACY RISKS

The term *privacy risk* is used in this book to refer to the *level of privacy* or the *privacy score* of an OSN profile as obtained by taking into account privacy harms, threats, risk sources, and attributes.

Privacy risk is measured in terms of the likelihood of privacy harms, that is, the probability that a privacy harm may be caused by the exploitation of attributes by risk sources. Thus, the privacy risk of the ith privacy harm h_i $(i = 1, \ldots, n)$ due to the decision $\mathbf{x}$ to reveal attributes is represented by $R_i(\mathbf{x}) : X \to \{a_i, 1\}$. Here, a_i $(0 \leq a_i < 1)$ represents the residual risk when the user does not reveal the attributes exploited to cause a harm and yet the risk source is able to infer them.

$R_i(\mathbf{x}) = 1$ if the harm h_i certainly occurs when decision $\mathbf{x}$ is taken. This happens when the user himself reveals attributes contributing to the harm. When the attributes leading to the harm can only be inferred because the user did not reveal them, then $R_i(\mathbf{x}) = a_i$. In this latter case, the risk exists only due to the vicinity.

The measure of privacy risk may be extended to include the proportion of attributes correctly inferred by risk sources so that users are able to gauge the future privacy problems that may arise from their OSN profiles.

A measure of privacy risk may also include information on the severity of a harm as assigned by a privacy expert. Severity can be defined as an estimation of the magnitude of potential impacts of privacy harms on users' privacy [32]. The French data protection authority CNIL provides a scale [34] to estimate severity.

2.7   PRIVACY RISK ANALYSIS

The myriad of information technology products and services deployed today rely heavily on the processing of personal data. The variety of personal data used by these systems is so large that they may lead to a lot of privacy harms negatively affecting users, in the absence appropriate protective measures.

To understand the privacy risks arising out of personal data processing, there is a growing consensus that a privacy impact assessment (PIA) should be conducted [43].

According to Wright and De Hert [154], a PIA is:

"a methodology for assessing the impacts on privacy of a project, policy, programme, service, product or other initiative which involves the processing of personal information and, in consultation with stakeholders, for taking remedial actions as necessary in order to avoid or minimize negative

impacts."

Clarke [30] defines PIA as:

"a process whereby the potential impacts and implications of proposals that involve potential privacy-invasiveness are surfaced and examined."

Several countries like the U.S., Canada, and the UK [155] have promoted the role of PIA. The EU GDPR [56] has also strongly emphasized on data protection impact assessments and has made it mandatory for certain types of data processing activities. A large body of literature that describe how PIA should be conducted already exists. The reader may refer to [45] for a review of this literature.

PRA forms the technical core of a PIA,[8] describing how privacy risks are to be computed [43]. PRA methodologies help the service provider to evaluate systems processing personal data for privacy risks, thus helping them to design and implement these systems in the least privacy invasive way. Very few works [39, 40, 42, 46], until now, have used PRA to directly help users assess and/or take actions to mitigate the risks of disclosing personal data.

Many works have focused on the details of PRA methodology, both for general personal data processing systems [26, 32–34, 48, 49, 60, 104, 156] as well as for specific ones, such as location-based systems, RFIDs, and smart grids [58, 59, 105]. However, only one of these methodologies, the LINDDUN risk analysis framework [49] provides an example of analyzing social networks. Later, PRA methodologies have also inspired privacy scoring of OSN profiles [39] and privacy settings management in OSNs [40, 42].

---

[8] A PIA process includes several steps such as planning, stakeholders consultation, resource allocation, audits, etc.

CHAPTER 3

Dimensions of Privacy Scoring in OSNs

As the need to inform OSN users about the privacy risks arising from sharing personal information is being increasingly appreciated, researchers have proposed various methods [5, 6, 8, 9, 15, 39, 95, 112, 116, 117, 132, 137, 147, 148, 150] to compute these risks and to present the result to users in terms of privacy scores.[1] The primary aim of these privacy scores is to increase the privacy awareness of the user about his information sharing actions.

Apart from the method of computing the privacy scores, privacy scoring mechanisms differ from each other across many basic dimensions:

- the type of data they analyze, attributes or posts;

- the assumptions they make about the user;

- the nature of privacy settings available to the user;

- the types of risk sources who may pose a privacy problem;

- different privacy metrics that contribute to the computation of the privacy score;

- the nature of data inference possibilities considered; and

- the countermeasures proposed with respect to the privacy scores.

This chapter discusses these basic dimensions. These are important considerations for any future work on privacy scoring in OSNs. Appendix B presents a comparison of some privacy scoring mechanisms.

3.1   TYPE OF DATA

An OSN user profile consists of the relatively static part comprising attributes as well as more dynamic data such as posts, likes and comments. Both these types of data deserve individual attention.

---

[1]Not all of these methods rely on privacy risk analysis concepts for computation of the privacy scores.

The static part is more or less constant in size and exhibit limited change over time. On the other hand, the dynamic part can be of varying size and newer values (posts, comments, etc.) are added over time.

Attributes help to introduce a user to other users of the OSN by expressing important personal information such as gender, education, workplace, interests, and so on. Therefore, many privacy scoring mechanisms pay attention solely to the privacy of each attribute [15, 95, 117] or sets of attributes leading to privacy harms [39] or the entire set of attributes [5, 15, 95, 117, 137].

Measuring the privacy risks of dynamic data such as posts or comments or messages is more complex in nature. A post, for example, can reveal a great deal of personal information not only about the user himself, but also about other users. Analysis of such unstructured, non-standard, and short snippets of text is still very difficult [148].

Whereas a single post may not always reveal much useful information about the user to a risk source, a series of posts can easily provide more comprehensive information about the user. Generally, privacy scoring methods consider the privacy risk of a single post or message at a time [8, 148]. Aghasian et al. [5] take into account the privacy of different information pieces such as address and interests extracted even from dynamic data of OSNs.

Although it is worthwhile to consider the static and dynamic parts separately, ultimately privacy scores must be associated with the entire user profile, to make the system fool-proof. This brings in further complexities as the interaction between these two parts of the user profile need to be considered whenever information is shared. The user may diligently try to hide his birth year from his contacts by not revealing this attribute, but a post on his birthday celebration (without the right privacy setting) can easily give away this personal information.[2]

From an even broader perspective, a composite privacy score could be associated with the information revealed across multiple OSNs [5] a user is a member of. Some risk sources, such as common contacts across several OSNs, have access to more information about the user than the latter may desire through aggregation of information available from all of these sources. For example, a user may not reveal his workplace on Facebook but do so on LinkedIn, whereas he may not reveal his political inclination on LinkedIn, but do so on Facebook. A common contact across these OSNs then may come to know both the pieces of information. The privacy settings of different OSNs may be different and therefore finding out common contacts and their levels of visbility across these OSNs is a complex task.

---

[2]An additional level of complexity is added when the posts and comments and the attributes shared by the users' contacts are also taken into consideration. Even though a user does not share his age, it can be inferred from the ages of his contacts. Similarly, a user may not share his birth day (B.Dt) with anyone but it can be inferred from a friend's post sharing photos of her birthday celebration. However, what friends share is neither a part of the user profile nor can be controlled by the user, with existing privacy controls.

3.2 ASSUMPTIONS ABOUT THE USER

Across different privacy scoring approaches, a variety of assumptions have been made about the users' privacy perceptions, understanding of data sensitivity, the effect of privacy harms, and so on. Some of these assumptions are as follows.

- Different users have different risk perceptions at varying layers (such as friends, friends-of-friends, etc.) of friendship [8, 9]. While some of them may be comfortable with their information being seen by friends-of-friends and beyond, others may be more protective about their information and would not like to share it beyond their friend circle.

- If the user prefers to disclose or has no problems in allowing the propagation of some data then it is less sensitive to him than if he prefers otherwise [95]. In other words, users have an understanding about the level of sensitiveness of different types of data to them and choose their privacy settings accordingly.

- The user understands the consequences of privacy harms (for example, identity theft may lead to financial loss) which is why they use a privacy scoring mechanism in the first place [39–41]. However, the user is not a privacy expert and hence does not understand the attribute combinations that lead to different harms. As a result, he may either disclose too little information on OSNs to derive any benefits or too much information making him highly vulnerable.

- The privacy attitudes toward different topics of posts varies across users [148]. If a user publishes a significant number of semi-private posts on a certain topic, he considers the topic to be less private. If he does not delete a post, then he does not regret publishing it.

3.3 PRIVACY SETTINGS

Two major types of privacy settings have been considered while computing privacy scores:

- a simple dichotomous setting [15, 40, 95, 137], where the user either keeps the information private or reveals it to the public, or

- a polytomous privacy setting [5, 41, 95], similar to that used in major OSNs like Facebook, allowing the user to keep an attribute fully private or reveal it to only friends, friends-of-friends or to the public.

3.4 RISK SOURCES

The risk of inappropriate disclosure of personal data varies with the type of audience. Generally, the audiences who may exploit the user's personal data are referred to as the adversary [148] or the attacker. Using the terminology of privacy risk analysis [43, 45], they can be referred to as risk sources (see definition in Chapter 2).

Other users of the OSN such as friends or followers of the user [39–41, 116, 148], friends-of-friends of the user [39–41, 116], and strangers [39–41, 116, 148] are the most common risk sources considered for privacy scoring. These risk sources account for a lot of common privacy harms. For example, a friend on an OSN user may be a colleague of the user and any negative impression gathered by him about the user from the OSN profile and/or posts can adversely affect the user in the workplace.

Third-party applications installed in the profiles of the friends of the target user have also been looked upon as a risk source [15, 137].

The OSN service provider who gets access to any data that the user uploads to the OSN, irrespective of the privacy settings used, may also be considered as the risk source as it can cause a wide number of privacy harms such as micro-targeting of advertisements and discrimination. In the Cambridge Analytica scandal, the OSN provider Facebook allowed the app "thisisyourdigitallife" to collect personal data of not only users who had used the app but also that of their friends without the latters' consent.

Similarly, advertisers and data brokers may also be considered as risk sources.

3.5   PRIVACY METRICS

A number of privacy metrics has been used to compute privacy scores. Among these, sensitivity, visibility, and reachability of information are some of the popular metrics.

3.5.1   SENSITIVITY

The more sensitive the revealed information, higher the privacy risk [95].

Across various privacy scoring mechanisms, the sensitivity of personal information shared in OSNs have often been considered to be user-defined. That is, users actively or passively indicate which personal information are sensitive to them.

Sensitivity values could be either given as input by the user for whom the privacy score is being computed or obtained from the knowledge of such values for an "average" user or estimated automatically from user chosen privacy settings of attributes [95, 117]. For example, most people try to protect highly sensitive information and hence users may be assumed to assign suitable privacy settings to sensitive attributes in his OSN profile [95]. In other words, a response matrix that records the privacy settings of different attributes by a number of users can be used to estimate the value of sensitivity of each attribute [95].

Wang and Nepali [150] assign sensitivity values which they call privacy impact factors to attributes based on a user survey. In the PScore framework [117], sensitivity is defined at the level of attribute values rather than attributes because for many attributes the sensitivity for one value may be different from that of another. For example, the sensitivity of the value "homosexual" may be higher for many users compared to the value "heterosexual."

On the other hand, sensitivity of personal data may be pre-defined by privacy experts depending on the privacy risks they may pose. The EU GDPR (Article 9 and Recital 51) [56] has defined a list of special category of data that includes personal data revealing racial or ethnic origin, political opinions, religious or philosophical beliefs, trade union memberships, genetic data, biometric data, data related to health, sex life, and sexual orientation. This type of data requires more protection than other personal data because they are "*by their nature, particularly sensitive in relation to fundamental rights and freedoms*" and "*as the context of their processing could create significant risks to the fundamental rights and freedoms*" (Recital 51, EU GDPR) [56] of the user.

3.5.2   VISIBILITY

The visibility of an attribute represents who in the OSN can see the attribute. It can be computed based on the privacy setting of the user [39, 95, 150]. Other factors that may affect visibility include attribute inference from the user's vicinity (depending on the privacy settings of the vicinity) [39], the ease of data extraction [5] and data reliability [5].

Very often, the visibility of an attribute is directly calculated from the privacy settings of the attribute. For example, in very simple terms, visibility of an attribute may be either 0 or 1, where a score of 0 means that the data is available only to the data owner and a score of 1 means it is available to everyone [117].

Similarly, the visibility of an attribute may also be considered to lie between 0 and 1, with 0 representing an unknown attribute, 1 representing a known attribute, and any value between 0 and 1 representing a partial disclosure of the attribute [150]. Such a modeling of visibility may be looked upon as the result of a polytomous privacy setting, where the user can hide the attribute completely (a value of 0) or reveal it to everybody (a value of 1) or only partially hide/reveal it (values between 0 and 1).

In Liu and Terzi's privacy scoring mechanism [95], the probability that an attribute is truly visible is estimated using the observed visibility values (i.e., the privacy settings) recorded in the response matrix using the Item Response Theory.

3.5.3   REACHABILITY

The notion of reachability describes the extent to which information shared by the user may spread in an OSN due to diffusion actions, such as re-sharing and commenting, on this information by other users [8]. Conceptually, reachability is different from visibility as the latter does not consider the effect of diffusion actions.

For social networks for which details of the information sharing activities may not be available, centrality metrics help to evaluate an OSN user's role in the information transmission process.

Related to reachability is the audience metric which represents the proportion of users at a certain layer of friendship who are expected to see some diffused information [9].

The user may be made aware about the privacy implications of revealing information by means of a privacy score estimated using the reachability and the audience metrics [8, 9]. The higher the reachability and audience, the higher the privacy risk of information sharing [9].

3.6   DATA INFERENCE

The user's social circle or vicinity can reveal many information about the user even if the user keeps these information private. For example, the user's age can be inferred from those of his friends. Thus, the risk source's capability to infer personal data have been taken into account in many privacy scoring mechanims [15, 39, 117].

For example, PrivAware [15] considers a very simple inference method where the most common value of an attribute revealed by the user's friend is considered to be the inferred attribute value of the user, if the number of friends who share this value exceeds a threshold. Risk sources who have access to more accurate inference methods can give rise to more privacy risks. Therefore, a privacy score computed based on a simple inference method as used in PrivAware can serve as a benchmark for the user.

Another approach is to consider all inference methods available and allow plugging in of new inference mechanisms to compute privacy scores [117] as and when desired.

3.7   SUGGESTION OF COUNTERMEASURES

Based on the computed privacy scores, users can be offered different countermeasures to reduce their privacy risks. Some countermeasures could be as follows:

- not sharing certain information which contribute to high privacy risk [40, 148];

- rating of the user's OSN friends based on their attitudes toward privacy, helping the user make an informed decision of sharing personal data with them [6, 116, 147];

- removing risky friends, such as friends with the highest number of common friends [15]; and

- choosing appropriate privacy settings for all the attributes [41].

The suggestion of countermeasures is not an easy task, especially for OSNs, from which users derive a lot of benefits. The most obvious countermeasures include restricting information disclosure and/or careful selection of friends, both of which may sharply decrease the benefits derived from the use of an OSN. Users need to choose the most appropriate countermeasures that provide them the optimal balance of benefits and privacy risks.

The problems of privacy risk evaluation and countermeasure selection, although linked, are both complex and merit independent attention.

CHAPTER 4

Attribute Visibility in OSN

The privacy settings of the target user and his vicinity contribute to the attributes that are visible about him [39]. Attributes may be visible to a risk source either because they are directly revealed to it by the user or because the risk source can infer their values based on the attributes disclosed by the user's vicinity.

Risk sources of different exploitation abilities based on the visibility of attributes, must be considered when computing the user's privacy risks. Failing to do so may result in wrong estimation of risks which, in turn, leads to the application of improper countermeasures.

If the user receives imprecise risk measurements then either he may be unwilling to share information on his OSN profile and hence lose out on benefits or he may share more information than he should making himself extremely vulnerable to harms. Therefore, it is very important to find out, at least to some degree of precision, which attributes are visible to which risk sources from the user as well as his vicinity. This chapter describes a method to do this.

4.1   VISIBILITY MATRIX

Any user in the OSN can use the privacy settings of an attribute in his OSN profile to restrict the audience from seeing its value. The information on the visibility of each attribute can be collected in the *visibility matrix* [39].

Each column of the visibility matrix refers to an attribute. The first row corresponds to the risk sources who can see the attributes from the target user's profile, based on his privacy setting. The remaining rows correspond to the risk sources who can see the attributes from his friends' profiles, based on their privacy settings. Thus, these remaining rows take care of the visibility of attributes due to the target user's vicinity.

Figure 4.1 shows Ana and her social circle in an OSN. Suppose, Ana does not want to reveal her birth year (B.Yr). However, Ana's friend Emma reveals her B.Yr to her friends. Emma has no mutual friend with Ana but has another friend Fabio. So when Emma discloses her B.Yr to her friends, it is visible to Ana and also to Fabio who is a friend-of-friend of Ana. No friend of Ana can see Emma's birth year. Therefore, the risk source $A.2$ (but not $A.1$) can observe the attribute B.Yr from Emma's profile. In this way, if Ana has many more friends whose B.Yr is visible to $A.2$, then this risk source can infer Ana's birth year.

The visibility matrix $\mathbb{M}$ of a target user T displays the visibility values of all attributes in $\mathbb{A}_D$ as given by their privacy settings chosen by the user and his friends.

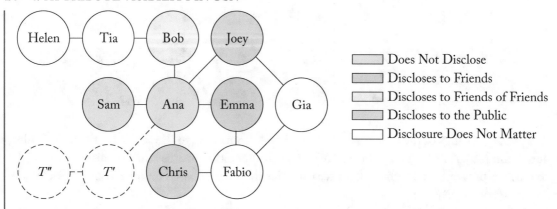

Figure 4.1: The target user, Ana, her vicinity, and the revelation of the attribute birth year B.Yr.

Each element of the visibility matrix is a set that denotes the members of the OSN to whom an attribute d in $\mathbb{A}_D$ is visible. These members are assigned based on the privacy setting of the attribute selected either by the user or a friend of the user.

The entry $\mathbb{M}[T, d]$ represents the visibility of the attribute d as set by T. We assume that $T_1 \in \mathbb{T}$ is a friend of T, where $\mathbb{T}$ is the set of T's friends. Then, the entry $\mathbb{M}[T_1, d]$ represents the visibility of attribute d as set by T_1, for any $T_1 \in \mathbb{T}$ (but, with respect to T and not themselves). Other types of privacy settings used in other OSNs can also be used to fill in $\mathbb{M}$.

To populate the visibility matrix, privacy settings of the user and his friends must be mined. Mining the privacy setting of the target user is easy, given the access to his profile. However, it is difficult to obtain the privacy settings of his friends as this information may be private. The next section describes a method that fills the visibility matrix, more or less precisely, overcoming this challenge.

4.2   CONSTRUCTION OF VISIBILITY MATRIX

This section describes the process of populating the visibility matrix with the help of Figures 4.2, 4.3, 4.4, and 4.5.

In these figures, each node represents an OSN user. Node T is the target user. Nodes T_1 and T_2 are his friends. Node T_3 is a friend of T_1. Node M_1 is a mutual friend of T and T_1. Similarly, M_3 is a mutual friend of T and T_3. Node N_1 is a non-mutual friend of T_1[1] and N_3 is a non-mutual friend of T_3. T' and T'' are dummy friend and friend-of-friend of T, respectively, and have been created for the purpose of constructing the visibility matrix of the target user T.

---

[1]A non-mutual friend refers to a friend who is not common to the target user and another friend of the target user. So, N_1 is not a common or mutual friend of T and T_1. He is only T_1's friend.

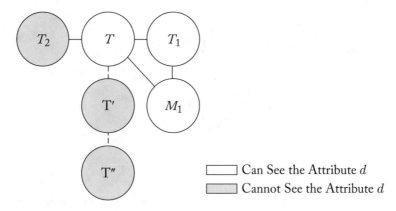

Figure 4.2: Attribute visibility when T_1's privacy setting is "friends" and T_1 has only a mutual friend M_1.

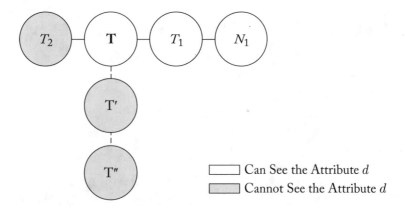

Figure 4.3: Attribute visibility when T_1's privacy setting is "friends" and T_1 has only non-mutual friend N_1.

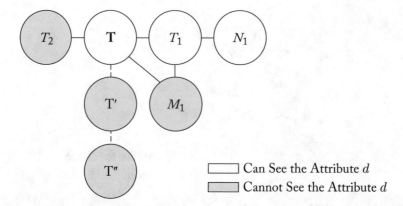

Figure 4.4: Attribute visibility when T_1's privacy setting is "friends" and T_1 has both mutual friend M_1 and non-mutual friend N_1.

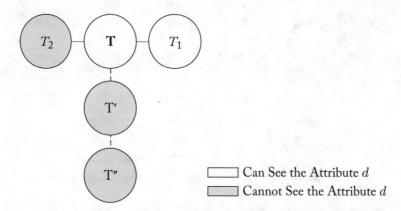

Figure 4.5: Attribute visibility when T_1's privacy setting is "friends" but has no friends except T.

In the figures, all real friendship links are depicted by solid lines between the nodes. Dummy friendship links (i.e., ones created artificially) are depicted by dotted lines between the nodes.

The first row of the visibility matrix concerns the privacy setting assigned by the user T himself. Thus, $\mathbb{M}[T, d]$ is assigned values as follows:

1. $\mathbb{M}[T, d] = \{\}$, if the privacy setting of d set by T is "private;"

2. $\mathbb{M}[T, d] = \{A.1\}$, if the privacy setting of d set by T is "friends;"

3. $\mathbb{M}[T, d] = \{A.1, A.2\}$, if the privacy setting of d set by T is "friends-of-friends;" and

4. $\mathbb{M}[T, d] = \{A.1, A.2, A.3\}$, if the privacy setting of d set by T is "public."

For every friend T_1 of T, the assignment of values to $\mathbb{M}[T_1, d]$ is more involved. To do this, one needs to know:

- the privacy settings of each friend in T's friendlist as well as

- in some cases, the friendlists of these friends and their friends.

Mining the privacy setting of the target user is easy when the mechanism is given access to his profile by the target user himself. However, it is difficult to obtain the privacy settings of his friends as having access to the user profile is not sufficient.

In order to visualize the privacy settings of T_1, the following dummy users are created:

- a dummy user T' who is a friend of T and

- a dummy user T'' who is a friend of the first dummy user T' and hence a friend-of-friend of T.

These two dummy users help to visualize the attribute visibility of each of T's friends.

The friendlists of T, T_1 and his friends may or may not be public. If they are not public, they are either private, i.e., not accessible or initially discarded for any information collection in order to reduce the mining step.

The visibility of the attribute d of a friend T_1 of T from T, T', and T'' may give rise to four cases.

Case 1. An attribute d of a friend T_1 is not visible from T, T', and T''.

Case 2. An attribute d of a friend T_1 is visible from T but not from T' and T''.

Case 3. An attribute d of a friend T_1 is visible from T and T' but not from T''.

Case 4. An attribute d of a friend T_1 is visible from T, T', and T''.

The visibility matrix $\mathbb{M}[T_1, d]$ is assigned values according to these four cases as described below. For the sake of brevity, Case 1 and Case 2 are discussed in details in this chapter. The interested reader can refer to Appendix C for a detailed description of Case 3 and Case 4.

Case 1. An attribute d of a friend T_1 is not visible from T, T', and T''. In this case, the privacy setting used by T_1 for d is "private" and hence, the corresponding cell in the visibility matrix $\mathbb{M}[T_1, d]$ is assigned an empty set.

Case 2. An attribute d of a friend T_1 is visible from T but not from T' and T''. In this case, the privacy setting used by T_1 for d is "friends." Now, the corresponding cell in the visibility matrix must be filled with the risk sources who can view T_1's attribute d from the point of view of T. To do this, one needs to check whether the friendlist of T_1 is public or not.

Scenario 1: Public Friendlist. If the friendlist is public, then the existence of mutual and non-mutual friends of T_1 with the target user T is checked. Then, the following four cases arise.

2.1.a. Only Mutual Friends. All friends of T_1 are also friends of T. In other words, T_1 has only mutual friend(s) with T. In this case, the attribute is visible only to the risk source $A.1$ (i.e., only to the mutual friends of T_1 and T) from T's perspective and so $\mathbb{M}[T_1, d]$ is assigned the value $\{A.1\}$. Figure 4.2 depicts this scenario. Although the attribute d is not visible to T_2 who is a friend of T, it is visible to M_1, the mutual friend of T_1 and T. This means that the attribute is visible to the risk source $A.1$, where $A.1$ comprises the mutual friends of T and T_1.

2.1.b. Only Non-mutual Friends. No friend of T_1 is a friend of T. In other words, there is no mutual friend between T_1 and T but T_1 has only non-mutual friend(s). In this case, the attribute is visible only to the risk source $A.2$ (i.e., only to the non-mutual friends of T_1 who are friends-of-friends with respect to T) from T's perspective and so $\mathbb{M}[T_1, d]$ is assigned the value $\{A.2\}$. Figure 4.3 depicts this scenario. Attribute d is not visible to T_2 who is a friend of T, but it is visible to N_1 who is a friend of T_1 but not a friend of T (i.e., non-mutual). This means that the attribute is visible to the risk source $A.2$, where $A.2$ comprises the non-mutual friends of T_1.

2.1.c. Both Mutual and Non-Mutual Friends. Some of T_1's friends are friends of T. In other words, T_1 has mutual friend(s) with T and also has non-mutual friend(s). In this case, the attribute is visible to the risk sources $A.1$ and $A.2$ (i.e., to the mutual friends of T_1 and T and to the non-mutual friends of T_1 who are friends-of-friends with respect to T) from T's perspective and so $\mathbb{M}[T_1, d]$ is assigned the value $\{A.1, A.2\}$. Figure 4.4 depicts this scenario. Although the attribute d is not visible to T_2 who is a friend of T, it is visible to M_1, the mutual friend of T_1 and T, and also to N_1 who is a friend of T_1 but not a friend of T (i.e., non-mutual). This means that the attribute is visible to the risk sources $A.1$ and $A.2$, where $A.1$ comprises the mutual friends of T and T_1 and $A.2$ comprises the non-mutual friends of T_1.

B.Yr

$$\begin{array}{cc} \text{Ana} & \\ \text{Bob} & \{A.1, A.2, A.3\} \\ \text{Chris} & \{A.1, A.2, A.3\} \\ \text{Emma} & \{A.2\} \\ \text{Joey} & \{A.1, A.2, A.3\} \\ \text{Sam} & \{\} \end{array}$$

Figure 4.6: Visibility matrix for the target user Ana for B.Yr.

2.1.d. Neither Mutual nor Non-Mutual Friends. T_1 has no friend other than T. In other words, there is no mutual friend between T_1 and T and T_1 has no non-mutual friend. In this case, the attribute is not visible to any risk source from T's perspective and so $\mathbb{M}[T_1, d]$ is assigned the value $\{\}$. Figure 4.5 depicts this scenario. Attribute d is not visible to anyone except T.

Scenario 2: Private Friendlist. If the friendlist of T_1 is private or cannot be collected, then the worst-case value $\{A.1, A.2\}$ is assigned to $\mathbb{M}[T_1, d]$.

The true visibility $Vis_{true}(T, d)$ of a target user's attribute d is the same as $\mathbb{M}[T, d]$.

4.3   AN ILLUSTRATION

This section illustrates how the visibility matrix is populated for a target user Ana, for the attribute birth year (B.Yr), given her friendship network and the disclosure of this attribute by her and her friends as shown in Figure 4.1.

In Figure 4.1, T' and T'' represent, respectively, the dummy friend and friend-of-friend of Ana introduced for the purpose of populating the visibility matrix. Since they are not real OSN users, their links to Ana and each other are represented by dotted lines in the figure. All real friendship links are denoted by solid lines.

Figure 4.6 presents Ana's visibility matrix. The first row of the matrix, $\mathbb{M}[Ana, B.Yr]$, corresponds to Ana's privacy setting for birth year. The subsequent rows represent the privacy settings of her friends (but, with respect to her) for birth year.

Ana's friend Emma reveals her birth year to her friends (since Ana, but not T' or T'', can see Emma's birth year). Emma has no mutual friends with Ana but has another friend Fabio. So when Emma discloses her birth year to her friends, it is visible to Ana and Fabio who is a friend-of-friend of Ana. No friend of Ana can see Emma's birth year. Therefore, in the visibility matrix, the row corresponding to Emma for birth year is filled up with the value $\{A.2\}$.

Ana's friend Bob reveals his birth year to his friends-of-friends (since Bob's birth year is visible from Emma and T' who is a friend of a friend for Bob, but not from T''). Bob has no mutual friends with Ana, but has a non-mutual friend Tia. Tia, in turn, does not have a mutual friend with Ana and has one non-mutual friend Helen. So, Bob's birth year is visible to Ana's friends (Chris, Emma, Joey, Sam), friends-of-friends (Tia) and strangers (Helen) with respect to Ana. So the corresponding cell in the visibility matrix is filled up with the value $\{A.1, A.2, A.3\}$.

Ana's friend Joey reveals his birth year to the public (i.e., beyond friend of friend, since Joey's birth year is visible from Emma, T' and T'' who is a stranger for Joey), i.e., $\{A.1, A.2, A.3\}$ with respect to Ana. Sam keeps his birth year private (since it is not visible from Ana). So, no risk sources can see Sam's birth year.

The true visibility of Ana's B.Yr is given by $Vis_{true}(v_{Ana}.B.Yr) = \{\}$.

4.4   OPEN PROBLEMS

The visibility of attributes, as discussed in this discourse, depends on the privacy settings of profile attributes set by the user and his friends. The discussion uses a generic privacy settings that includes keeping an attribute private or revealing it to friends, friends-of-friends or to the public. The method for populating the visibility matrix may be adapted to take into account the privacy settings of specific OSNs. For example, at present, Facebook allows a user to reveal an attribute to a specific set of friends or to all friends except a specific set of friends.

The notion of visibility described so far depends on the assumption that the user's vicinity constitutes friends in his friendlist. From the point of view of risk sources, the user's friendlist may not be always accessible as he may keep it private. In such cases, the risk source may try to infer friendship links between users and other members of the OSN from the public friendlists of these members [2] and based on other users who react to the target user's posts and comments. This may lead to the risk source building a broader vicinity that may consist of not only the user's friends but also friends of friends. The risk source may then use the attributes revealed by this broader vicinity to infer the attribute values of the user. Therefore, it is worthwhile to conceptualize a method to simulate the vicinity re-constructing actions of the risk source and incorporate this re-constructed vicinity into the construction of the visibility matrix.

CHAPTER 5

Harm Trees for OSNs

The personal data disclosed by users in OSN profiles in terms of attributes can be exploited by other OSN members (e.g., complete strangers, future employers, colleagues, and relatives) to cause various privacy harms such as identity theft, discrimination, or sexual predation for the OSN user.

Thus, users face privacy risks from privacy harms due to the exploitation of attributes revealed in their profile and their friends' profiles by risk sources. Although users may understand the negative consequences of privacy harms such as identity theft and stalking, they usually lack the expertise to link attribute revelation to these harms. However, this relationship is crucial in order to evaluate the risks of the user's OSN profile.

In this chapter, we turn our attention to describing harm trees that establish this relationship. Harm trees constitute an essential element in privacy risk analysis based scoring of OSN profiles and privacy setting management.

5.1 HARM TREES

The relationship among the attributes exploited by various risk sources, the threats, and a privacy harm can be graphically represented in the form of a tree-structure called *harm tree*. Harm trees are conceptually similar to attack trees in the computer security literature [83, 84, 124, 125, 157].

The concept is not entirely new in the context of privacy and privacy risk analysis [39, 43–45, 47, 49, 59, 102]. Harm trees, linking privacy weaknesses[1] and risk sources to harms via feared events,[2] have been used to compute the harm likelihood in the PRA methodology proposed in [45].

Other equivalent tree structures have also been used in privacy risk analysis. The LIND-DUN framework [49, 156] uses threat trees to link threats such as unjustifiable or excessive data collection and inappropriate use of data to vulnerabilities in a system. In the context of location-based systems, Friginal et al. [59] use attack trees to link what they define as adverse impacts (such as disclosure of nearest friends of an user) to attack scenarios (such as hacking a device).

Harm trees have been used for the evaluation of privacy scores and to aid users in privacy management in OSNs [39, 40, 42]. They establish the link between the exploitation of attributes by risk sources and the occurrence of a particular harm.

In all these cases, it is the job of the privacy expert to construct the harm trees.

---

[1]Privacy weaknesses are weaknesses in the data protection mechanism or lack thereof [45].
[2]*Feared event* is a notion that is similar to threats defined in this book.

The harm tree representation is beneficial both for the privacy expert and the target user. The graphical structure enables privacy experts to visually construct, update, delete, and view harm trees by choosing different logical connectors (AND, OR, etc.), declaring threats, risk sources, and attributes. In addition, the computation of privacy risks can be based on harm trees, re-using existing techniques of computing attack likelihoods using attack trees [157]. Other interesting features of attack trees, such as the linking of counter-measures to the tree nodes, can also be used to enrich harm trees.

The target user, although aware of the consequences of privacy harms, often lacks the expertise to link the revelation of multiple attributes to privacy harms. They can easily visualize this relationship through harm trees. A simplified, explanatory version of the harm tree can contribute to the user's comprehension of which attributes must not be disclosed and why, while trying to protect himself from a privacy harm.

5.2   CONSTRUCTION OF HARM TREES

The root node of a harm tree denotes a privacy harm. Leaf nodes represent the exploitation of user attributes by risk sources. Intermediate nodes represent threats or personal data exploited by risk sources to accomplish the harm.

Child nodes can be connected by:

1. an AND node if all of them are necessary to give rise to the parent node, or

2. an OR node if any one of them is sufficient to give rise to the parent node.

The harm tree in Figure 5.1 represents that the user's profile can be assessed for stalking (h_1) by strangers ($A.3$). The stalker can utilize the user's gender (Gen) or age (Age) to assess the profile. He also needs to know a more or less precise location of the user given by either the home locality (H.Loc) derived from the attribute home address (H.Add) or the work locality (W.Loc) derived from the attribute workplace (W.Pl). These information can be accessed directly or inferred (FE.1) by the risk source.

Figure 5.2 represents that identity theft (h_3) can be caused by the access to data (FE.1) by strangers ($A.3$). Birth year (B.Yr) and birthday (B.Dt) (which together give date of birth or DoB), home address (H.Add), and phone number (Ph.) are necessary to cause this harm.

5.2.1   HARM LIKELIHOOD

For computation of harm likelihoods based on harm trees, different sets of rules may be used. For example, in [45], the following rules have been used:

R1. AND node with independent child nodes: $p = \Pi_i \, p_i$

R2. AND node with dependent child nodes: $p = Min_i \, p_i$

R3. OR node with independent child nodes: $p = 1 - (\Pi_i(1 - p_i))$

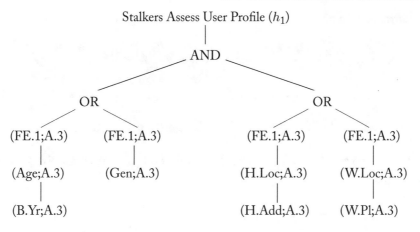

Figure 5.1: Harm tree for "stalkers assess user profile" (h_1).

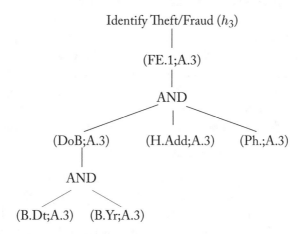

Figure 5.2: Harm tree for "identity theft/fraud" (h_3).

R4. OR node with dependent child nodes: $p = Min(1, \sum_i p_i)$

In [41], the following rules have been used to evaluate the likelihoods:

R1. AND node: $p = Min_i \, p_i$ [3]

R2. OR node: $p = Max_i \, p_i$

---

[3] If the child nodes are independent only then the probability p_{AND} associated with an AND node can be represented by $\prod_i p_i$. Such an assumption need not be made when considering min. Irrespective of independence, the joint probability of the child nodes is always less than or equal the minimum of the probabilities of all the child nodes ($\min_i (p_i)$) [157]. So, by choosing, min one over-approximates the probability at the AND node and hence also the harm likelihoods.

Table 5.1: Harm expressions

Code	Harm Expressions
h_1	$\min(\max(y_{B.Yr,A.3}, y_{Gen,A.3}), \max(y_{W.Pl,A.3}, y_{H.Add,A.3}))$
h_3	$\min(\min(y_{B.Dt,A.3}, y_{B.Yr,A.3}), y_{H.Add,A.3}, y_{Ph.,A.3}) =$ $\min(y_{B.Dt,A.3}, y_{B.Yr,A.3}, y_{H.Add,A.3}, y_{Ph.,A.3})$

In both the above cases, p is the likelihood of a node and p_i is the likelihood of its ith child node.

5.3   HARM EXPRESSIONS

For a given user profile, a privacy harm presents a risk with a certain likelihood. When this risk is computed, one must consider that: the user may or may not reveal an attribute d presented by the leaf node of a harm tree at a level l, where l coincides with the risk source that needs to exploit the attribute to cause the harm. This decision of the user is denoted by the variable $x_{d,l}$, where $x_{d,l} = 1$ if the attribute is revealed and $x_{d,l} = 0$ otherwise.

When a user reveals an attribute, i.e., $x_{d,l} = 1$, the value is known for certain; otherwise, it is known only with an accuracy $Acc(l, d)$, where $Acc(l, d)$ is the accuracy of inferring attribute d from the user's vicinity and $0 \leq Acc(l, d) < 1$.

Therefore, each leaf node of a harm tree can be represented by another variable $y_{d,l}$ where

$$y_{d,l} = Max(x_{d,l}, Acc(l, d)). \tag{5.1}$$

Each harm tree can be represented as a *harm expression* in terms of $y_{d,l}$, where an *AND* node is replaced by the min function and an *OR* node is replaced by the max function.

The likelihood of the harm occurring is then evaluated by using the harm expression. For example, the harm tree in Figure 5.1 can be presented as the following harm expression:

$$\min(\max(y_{B.Yr,A.3}, y_{Gen,A.3}), \max(y_{W.Pl,A.3}, y_{H.Add,A.3})). \tag{5.2}$$

Table 5.1 presents the harm expressions for the harms stalking (h_1) and identity theft (h_2). The expressions for other harms are similar.

The accuracy values $Acc(l, d)$ can be computed using different methods [39, 161], for example the friend-aggregate model in [161]. Other types of computations of the accuracy value are also possible, depending upon the inference method being used.

Harm expressions can be used to evaluate the privacy risk of the user's profile.

5.4   HARM DATABASE

Harm trees may be constructed by privacy experts before a risk evaluation process and stored in the harm database. The latter can be updated when new harms are discovered. Existing harm trees can also be modified based on new information. This procedure can be performed once (and the database can be updated once in a while) and can be reused for the risk evaluation for each target user and even for different OSNs.

The construction of new harm trees or the process of updating existing ones can be based on research in privacy and security in OSNs that discuss new types of privacy harms and attribute exploitation by risk sources based on existing and new features of the OSN.

5.5   OPEN PROBLEMS

Harm trees, in the context of privacy scoring and privacy settings management in OSNs, can be enhanced in many ways, some of which are discussed in this section.

The harm trees described in this discourse only consider a limted set of privacy harms, threats, risk sources, and data. Other privacy harms, threats such as re-sharing of data, risk sources such as OSN service providers and advertisers, and personal data extracted from comments and posts can be included to enhance the harm trees and hence the privacy scores. In addition, different capabilities of risk sources such as the availability of background knowledge such as personal data available from sources other than the OSN under consideration, can be incorporated in the construction and evaluation of harm trees and harm expressions.

The leaf nodes of the harm trees described here denote the exploitation of data that risk sources get access to. In other words, leaf nodes signify the exploitation of the inappropriate usage of existing privacy settings by the user and his vicinity. However, risks may originate due to a weakness in the privacy setting itself or in general other privacy protective mechanisms offered by the OSN. For example, the privacy settings considered in the book does not allow users to hide data from specific friends. These weaknesses in privacy protection mechanisms should also be considered when harm trees are constructed.

CHAPTER 6

Privacy Risk Analysis in OSNs

The EU GDPR [56] emphasizes that data subjects should be made aware of the risks related to personal data processing. In general, privacy impact assessment (PIA), whose technical core is referred to as privacy risk analysis (PRA) [45], is used to help service providers understand the privacy risks for data subjects from services they provide. With the GDPR coming into force in May 2018, it has become mandatory to conduct such assessments for certain kinds of personal data processing in Europe.

It is possible to use the privacy risk analysis approach to inform users about the privacy risks of their choices of privacy settings when revealing their personal data in OSNs. Knowledge of the risk arising out of current privacy settings can nudge users toward choosing more privacy-preserving settings for their attributes.

This chapter highlights how the main concepts of privacy risk analysis, such as privacy harms, risk sources, threats, and harm trees [39, 45], can be used to develop a privacy scoring mechanism. In contrast to traditional PRA, such a privacy scoring mechanism is meant to help users, instead of service providers, to understand the privacy risks of data sharing in OSNs. This discourse is based on the PRA-based privacy scoring mechanism called PrivOSN.[1]

The privacy scores help users understand the privacy risks presented by their OSN profiles due to the current privacy settings of their profile attributes and their vicinity. Methods like PrivOSN can also be utilized in broader privacy management mechanisms to arrive at the optimal privacy settings for the attributes, helping the user to preserve privacy as well as the benefits of participation in the OSN.

6.1   AN OVERVIEW

The personal data disclosed by users in OSN profiles in terms of attributes can be exploited by other OSN members, including complete strangers, future employers, colleagues, and relatives to cause various privacy harms such as identity theft, discrimination or sexual predation, for the user. A privacy scoring mechanism is primarily used to make the user aware of the privacy risks they face from such privacy harms due to the attributes revealed in their profile and their friends' profiles.

The user does not know how different attributes, alone or in combination with others, can lead to these harms when exploited by risk sources. Thus, as the starting point of PrivOSN, pri-

---

[1]A preliminary version of this work [39] appeared in the Proceedings of the 12th International Conference on Risks and Security of Internet and Systems, 2017.

vacy expert(s) build the *harm trees* and the *harm database*, of known privacy harms (see Chapter 5 on how to construct harm trees and harm databases). For example, strangers ($A.3$) can exploit a target user's birth day (B.Dt), birth year (B.Yr), phone number (Ph), and home address (H.Add) for identity theft. Similarly, a target user may face social isolation when his colleagues ($A.1$) come to know about his political (Pol) or religious views (Rel) or sexual orientation (G.Int).

Generally, a user reveals only some of the attributes in his profile to any risk source while the others remain hidden. Similarly, his friends only reveal some attributes and hide others from this risk source. The visibility of different attributes to different risk sources can be obtained from the *visibility matrix* (see Chapter 4 for a description on how to construct the visibility matrix). The risk source, in turn, tries to find out the hidden attributes based on the user's vicinity.

In other words, given the set of partially filled OSN profiles of the user and his friends $\mathbb{P}_k = \{P_{T,k}, P_{1,k}, \ldots, P_{m,k}\}$ (where $P_{T,k}$ denotes the profile of the target user and $P_{i,k}$ the profile of the ith friend, $i = 1, \ldots, m$ as viewed by the risk source $A.k$ at the given level k, $k = 1, 2, 3$), a risk source $A.k$ can find out the profile of the target user $P_{V,T,k}$ in which all hidden attributes have been assigned values inferred from the attributes revealed in the profiles $P_{1,k}, \ldots, P_{m,k}$ in $\mathbb{P}_k$.

Different types of inference methods may be used by the risk source. Based on this, the risk source may have different levels of confidence with the inferred data. This confidence level is referred to as the *accuracy* of the inferred attribute.

$P_{V,T,k}$ is referred to as the *virtual profile* because the inferred attribute values may or may not be correct. Suppose, there exists a *real profile* consisting of all correct attribute values of the target user and denoted by $P_{R,T}$. Depending on the number of attributes correctly inferred, $P_{V,T,k}$ may coincide with $P_{R,T}$ when all attributes have been correctly inferred or it may be different when some attributes are not correctly inferred.

An example of $P_{R,T}$ and $P_{V,T,3}$ with respect to risk source $A.3$ is shown in Table 6.1. In this example, the user reveals his phone number (Ph) and home address (H.Add) to strangers and keeps other attributes hidden. So, a risk source $A.3$ has access to the correct values of only these attributes. $A.3$ tries to infer the rest of the attributes based on the values revealed by the user's vicinity.

In Table 6.1, in the real profile ($P_{R,T}$), all attribute values are correctly known. Therefore, a comparison with the virtual profile $P_{V,T,k}$ can show which attributes have been correctly inferred by $A.3$ and which ones are incorrectly inferred. So, it can be said that $A.3$ correctly infers some of the attributes, for example, birth year (B.Yr), workplace (W.Pl), religious orientation (Rel), relationship status (RStat), gender (Gen), and interests (Int). However, he incorrectly infers the other attributes, gender interest (G.Int) and political affiliation (Pol). In addition, even if the vicinity reveals their birth days, $A.3$ cannot infer the attribute birth day (B.Dt) of the user, which therefore remains unknown to him.

The closer the virtual profile is to the real profile, the higher is the risk because the risk source then acts on a larger number of correctly inferred attribute values. However, the user

Table 6.1: Real and virtual profiles of target user T ("?" denotes that an attribute has been hidden by the user from strangers ($A.3$), "✓" denotes that the attribute is revealed by the user, "✓ ✓" denotes that the attribute has been correctly inferred, "×" denotes that the attribute has been incorrectly inferred, "−" denotes that the attribute cannot be inferred)

All Attributes	Attributes Values in $P_{R,\,T}$	Attributes Revealed/ Hidden by T from Strangers ($A.3$)	Attributes Revealed/ Inferred in $P_{V,T,3}$
B.Yr	1984	?	1984 (✓✓)
B.Dt	April 12	?	−
Gen	Male	?	Male (✓✓)
Ph	8563421	8563421 (✓)	8563421 (✓)
G.Int	Female	?	Male (×)
H.Add	23 Avenue Leclerc 32000 Kansas	23 Avenue Leclerc 32000 Kansas (✓)	23 Avenue Leclerc 32000 Kansas (✓)
W.Pl	ICICI, Kansas	?	ICICI, Kansas (✓✓)
Pol	Left	?	Center (×)
Rel	Atheist	?	Atheist (✓✓)
RStat	Single	?	Single (✓✓)
Int	Swimming	?	Swimming (✓✓)

may also suffer from privacy harms, due to incorrectly inferred attributes. For example, if the target user is male but has been inferred to be a female, then he can suffer from discriminations intended toward females and vice versa. So, PrivOSN takes into account such scenarios when computing privacy risks, but leaves it to the target user to decide whether they are interesting to him.

The risk for a harm is presented in terms of a measure of the *harm likelihood* as well as a measure for similarity between the real and virtual profiles, referred to as *profile similarity*. Harm likelihood computation depends on the accuracy of inference of the concerned attributes and the harm trees. Profile similarity is an indicator of the scopes of future privacy risks.

6.2   PRIVOSN IN DETAILS

PrivOSN requires very little user interaction. A target user must provide a pointer to his OSN profile to let the mechanism access the privacy settings of different attributes set by him and his friendlist.

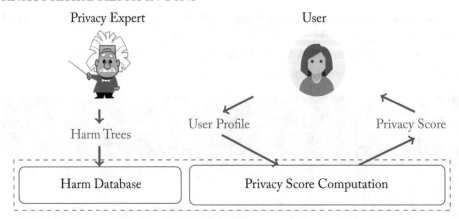

Figure 6.1: An overview of PrivOSN.

This input is enough to compute a basic form of harm likelihoods and no other input is required from the user. However, if a user is willing to give PrivOSN access to the actual attribute values, i.e., the access to the real profile $P_{R,T}$, then harm likelihoods can be computed based on these actual values.

Profile similarity may be computed in two ways. The user may give PrivOSN access to the real profile and obtain the value of the profile similarity directly. However, users may not be comfortable sharing their real attribute values with the mechanism. In such a case, they may choose to compute the profile similarity themselves.

Figure 6.1 provides a visual overview of PrivOSN. In a nutshell, this privacy risk analysis based method to compute privacy scores of OSN profiles consists of performing the following steps:

1. construction of *harm trees* and *harm databases* by privacy experts;

2. construction of the *visibility matrix*;

3. computation of the *accuracy* of inferred attribute values;

4. evaluation of *harm likelihoods* based on accuracy values and harm trees;

5. computation of *profile similarity*; and

6. presentation of evaluated *privacy risks* to the user in terms of the likelihood and similarity measure. Alternatively, the computed likelihoods can be fed into a mechanism to choose the optimal privacy settings.

Chapters 4 and 5 have already discussed how to build the visibility matrix and harm trees, respectively. So, this section begins to describe the process from the third step, i.e., the computation of accuracy values. It also discusses how the privacy risks are presented to the users.

$$\begin{array}{cc} & \text{B.Yr} \\ \begin{array}{c} \text{Ana} \\ \text{Bob} \\ \text{Chris} \\ \text{Emma} \\ \text{Joey} \\ \text{Sam} \end{array} & \begin{pmatrix} \{\} \\ \{A.1, A.2, A.3\} \\ \{A.1, A.2, A.3\} \\ \{A.2\} \\ \{A.1, A.2, A.3\} \\ \{\} \end{pmatrix} \end{array}$$

Figure 6.2: Visibility matrix for the target user Ana for B.Yr.

Chapter 8 will show how the computed likelihoods can be used to choose an optimal privacy setting for the user.

6.2.1   COMPUTATION OF ACCURACY

An attribute poses a risk to the target user when either it is revealed by him or it is inferred from his vicinity with a high accuracy by a risk source.

The computation of accuracy varies based on whether the attribute is revealed by the target user himself. The information on whether an attribute is made visible to a particular risk source by the target user himself or by his friends is available from the visibility matrix (as discussed in Chapter 4).

As an illustration, for the target user Ana, the visibility matrix in Figure 6.2 shows that Ana does not reveal her birth year to the risk source $A.2$. However, $A.2$ can infer Ana's birth year from the birth years visible to it from her vicinity, i.e., from the profiles of her friends Bob, Chris, Emma, and Joey.

When the target user T himself reveals an attribute d to a risk source $A.k$ ($k = 1, 2, 3$), i.e., if $A.k \in Vis_{true}(T, d)$, then its true value is known with full confidence by the risk source. In this case, the accuracy of the attribute d is given as: $Acc(A.k, d) = 1$.

When the target user does not reveal the attribute, it has to be inferred. However, inference is possible only when the relevant attributes are visible to the risk source $A.k$ from the vicinity.

PrivOSN considers that a simple inference method based on the data collected from the vicinity, is used by the risk source. The value of an attribute that is most common among the user's vicinity is assumed to be the inferred value of the attribute. It is also possible to use more precise inference methods, but such methods require the development of inference patterns (such as attribute d_1 can be inferred from attribute d_2 and so on) and their validation on large offline datasets. By choosing the simple inference technique, such complexities can be avoided and one can enable fast, online computation of the privacy risks.

An attribute d can assume many values. The ith value of d is represented as d_{v_i}. The accuracy is computed over all such values revealed by the vicinity.[2] It is computed as the proportion of the vicinity who reveals the most common value (i.e., the most frequent value among the user's friends) of the attribute.

More precisely, the accuracy of d is computed by the risk source $A.k$ as the maximum over the ratios of the number of friends ($n_{d=d_{v_i}}$) of the target user who reveals to $A.k$ each value d_{v_i} and the total number of his friends (n_d) who reveal attribute d. This is given by:

$$Acc(A.k, d) = Max_{d_{v_i}} \frac{n_{d=d_{v_i}}}{n_d}. \tag{6.1}$$

This accuracy value is then used to compute the harm likelihood.

If the user is willing to reveal the values of his attributes to PrivOSN, then the true value of d for the target user is available to PrivOSN and is denoted by d_{true}. The *accuracy* can then be computed as the proportion of the vicinity who reveals the true value of the attribute.

In this case, the accuracy is computed as the ratio of the number of friends ($n_{d=d_{true}}$) of the target user who reveal to $A.k$ the true value d_{true} of the attribute d and the total number of his friends (n_d) who reveal the attribute d. Thus, real accuracy of d is given by:

$$Acc_r(A.k, d) = \frac{n_{d=d_{true}}}{n_d}. \tag{6.2}$$

One can then use this accuracy value for the computation of harm likelihoods.

If d_{true} is not among the values d_{v_i} revealed by the vicinity, then $Acc_r(A.k, d) = 0$.

6.2.2   EVALUATION OF HARM LIKELIHOODS

Harm likelihood can be evaluated based on *harm expressions* that are derived using the method described in Chapter 5.

Suppose that the user reveals their home address (H.Add) to strangers (A.3) but their birth year (B.Yr), gender (Gen), and workplace (W.Pl) only to their friends (A.1). However, the vicinity of the user reveals their birth years, genders, and workplaces even to strangers. Thus, from the vicinity $A.3$ has inferred the birth year, gender, and workplace with the following accuracies[3]:

$$Acc(A.3, B.Yr) = 0.8, \tag{6.3}$$
$$Acc(A.3, Gen) = 0.6, \tag{6.4}$$
$$Acc(A.3, W.Pl) = 0.4. \tag{6.5}$$

---

[2]It is possible that certain attributes can assume values other than that revealed by the vicinity. For example, a certain target user's vicinity may reveal that they work in workplaces (W.Pl) A, B, C, and D. Of course, it is still possible that this attribute may have other values in reality. But, while computing the accuracy of an undisclosed attribute, it is considered that the attribute can only assume one of the values revealed by the vicinity. For the example of the attribute workplace, it is assumed that the values of W.Pl may be only A, B, C, or D.

[3]The values of some attributes such as phone number (Ph.) and birth day (B.Dt) cannot be inferred from the vicinity.

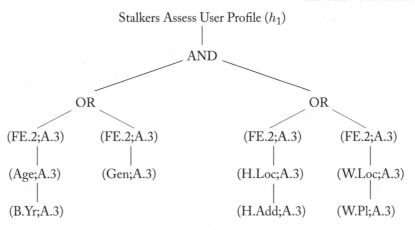

Figure 6.3: Harm tree for "stalkers assess user profile" (h_1).

The harm expression corresponding to the harm "stalkers assess user profile" (h_1) described in Figure 6.3 is:

$$\min(\max(y_{B.Yr,A.3}, y_{Gen,A.3}), \max(y_{H.Add,A.3}, y_{W.Pl,A.3})). \qquad (6.6)$$

Therefore, the likelihood of the user becoming a victim of stalking (h_1) is:

$$\min(\max(y_{B.Yr,A.3}, y_{Gen,A.3}), \max(y_{H.Add,A.3}, y_{W.Pl,A.3})) = 0.8, \qquad (6.7)$$

where

$$y_{B.Yr,A.3} = \max(x_{B.Yr,A.3}, Acc(A.3, B.Yr)) = \max(0, 0.8) = 0.8, \qquad (6.8)$$
$$y_{Gen,A.3} = \max(x_{Gen,A.3}, Acc(A.3, Gen)) = \max(0, 0.6) = 0.6, \qquad (6.9)$$
$$y_{H.Add,A.3} = x_{H.Add,A.3} = 1, \qquad (6.10)$$
$$y_{W.Pl,A.3} = \max(x_{W.Pl,A.3}, Acc(A.3, W.Pl)) = \max(0, 0.4) = 0.4. \qquad (6.11)$$

The likelihoods for other harms can be similarly computed.

6.2.3   COMPUTATION PROFILE SIMILARITY

Profile similarity ($P_{s,k}$), for a given risk source, is simply computed as the ratio of the number of attributes that the risk source $A.k$ managed to infer correctly ($n_{c,k}$), to the total number of

Table 6.2: An example of privacy risks as presented to the target user T

Code	Privacy Harm	Harm Likelihood	Profile Similarity for A.3 $(P_{s,3})$
h_1	Stalking	0.8	
h_2	Job screening	0.9	0.75
h_3	Identity theft	0	

attributes that has not been revealed to this risk source by the target user $(n_{a,k})$.[4] Thus,

$$P_{s,k} = \frac{n_{c,k}}{n_{a,k}}. \tag{6.12}$$

To illustrate, for the real and virtual profiles in Table 6.1, $P_{s,k} = 0.75$ as six out of eight unrevealed attributes (excluding B.Dt) have been correctly inferred.

PrivOSN can compute the profile similarity itself when it has access to the real profile of the user allowing it to determine the number of correctly inferred attributes $(n_{c,k})$. If the user does not reveal his real profile, then PrivOSN provides the user with the virtual profile $P_{V,T,3}$ after flagging all inferred values.[5] The user then compares the inferred values with the correct values of attributes to find out the number of correctly inferred values $(n_{c,k})$ and can compute the profile similarity himself.[6]

$P_{s,k}$ contributes to a measure of potential privacy risks in terms of correctly inferred attributes that can be used to cause harms in the future, when the vicinity of the user changes or new harms using these correctly inferred attributes are added to the harm database. Thus, it is an indicator of future problems.

6.2.4 PRESENTATION OF PRIVACY RISK TO THE USER

The target user is presented with the likelihood of each harm and the profile similarity $(P_{s,k})$ for each risk source $A.k$ as the measure of the privacy risk from his OSN profile.

In addition, the curious target user can request to see the list of all attributes that have been correctly inferred in their profiles. This helps the target user to take appropriate countermeasures with respect to the correctly inferred attributes.

To illustrate, Table 6.2 depicts the measures of privacy risk presented to the target user.

For any target user, the higher the profile similarity and harm likelihood, higher is his privacy risk. Suppose, the harm likelihoods for the three harms stalking (h_1), job screening (h_2) and identity theft (h_3) are 0.8, 0.9, and 0, respectively (see Table 6.2). Then, job screening (h_2)

---

[4] $n_{a,k}$ does not include attributes that cannot be inferred from the vicinity, for example birth day (B.Dt).
[5] Flagging of inferred values is necessary because users may not remember which attributes he has revealed at what level.
[6] The number of flagged values gives the value of $n_{a,k}$.

is the harm that should concern the user more than any other harm. The profile similarity for $A.3$ ($P_{s,3} = 0.75$) shows that $A.3$ has correctly inferred 75% of the attributes not revealed by the user.

The correct inference of the attributes is an indicator of future privacy risks. For example, if in the future the user decides to reveal B.Dt to $A.3$, he may become the victim of identity theft as he has already revealed Ph and H.Add to $A.3$ and $A.3$ has correctly inferred B.Yr, given there are no other changes. In addition, profile similarity also indicates the potential risk if new harms concerning one or more of the correctly inferred attributes are discovered. Thus, higher the value of profile similarity, higher is the risk.

6.3   RESIDUAL RISKS

Since the attributes revealed by the user's vicinity can be used to reveal those of the user and the user's privacy setting cannot be used to prevent such inference, a residual risk may always exist [161] even if the user does not reveal the attributes contributing to the harm(s).

This residual risk for the harm h_i can be denoted by a_i, where $0 \leq a_i < 1$. When the vicinity is not useful to infer the attributes contributing to the harm h_i, then $a_i = 0$, otherwise $a_i > 0$. Unless the user himself reveals an attribute, that attribute can never be known for sure, no matter what the vicinity reveals. Thus, the residual risk a_i is the likelihood of the harm h_i occurring when none of the attributes contributing to that harm is revealed by the target user himself.

In other words, the residual risk denotes the likelihood of the harm when the attributes contributing to the harm can only be inferred from the vicinity. It can be computed using the harm expressions derived in Chapter 5.

Using the example in Section 6.2.2, the residual risk a_1 for the harm stalking (h_1) for the user can be computed as follows:

$$a_1 = \min(\max(y_{B.Yr,A.3}, y_{Gen,A.3}), \max(y_{H.Add,A.3}, y_{W.Pl,A.3})) = 0.4, \qquad (6.13)$$

where

$$y_{B.Yr,A.3} = \max(x_{B.Yr,A.3}, acc_{B.Yr,A.3}) = \max(0, 0.8) = 0.8, \qquad (6.14)$$

$$y_{Gen,A.3} = \max(x_{Gen,A.3}, acc_{Gen,A.3}) = \max(0, 0.6) = 0.6, \qquad (6.15)$$

$$y_{H.Add,A.3} = x_{H.Add,A.3} = 0, \qquad (6.16)$$

$$y_{W.Pl,A.3} = \max(x_{W.Pl,A.3}, acc_{W.Pl,A.3}) = \max(0, 0.4) = 0.4 \qquad (6.17)$$

(since for residual risk computation, it is assumed that the user does not reveal any attributes).

6.4   OPEN PROBLEMS

The privacy risk-based scoring of OSN profiles discussed in this chapter opens several new interesting research directions.

An immediate enhancement of the privacy scoring mechanism would be to include severity of the privacy harms in the computation of privacy risks. Traditionally, many privacy risk analysis methods consider the severity of harms as an important factor. The severity values may follow a pre-defined scale, for example, the one proposed by the French data protection authority CNIL [34]. These values may also be decided based on user surveys, taking into account the fact that some privacy harms may affect different groups of users differently.

The privacy scoring mechanism can also be extended to take into account dynamic data and the context of specific OSNs.

Another interesting extension of the mechanism would be to adapt it for estimating the privacy risks arising from multiple OSNs, by taking into account a larger variety of harms, risk sources, attributes, and privacy settings related to these OSNs. The notion of the user's vicinity must also be updated accordingly.

The privacy scoring mechanism discussed here uses only a simple inference method at present. However, other inference methods may also be used. The computation of the accuracy values would change accordingly. In fact, similar to the harm database, privacy experts can create a database of inference methods available for all attributes concerned, based on existing research in the area. This would signify that risk sources, of different capabilities, may choose an appropriate inference method from the database. A more precise privacy score can then be computed by plugging in the appropriate accuracy value, based on the chosen inference method, to the main computation process. Like the harm database, privacy experts can update the database of inference methods as and when new inference methods come to light.

In addition, the model can be made more realistic by considering that:

- the target user's friendlist may contain ties of different strengths leading to a more fine-grained list of risk sources;

- a risk source can gain access to data that has been re-shared by another risk source who has direct access to it; and

- extra information about a target user, available to risk sources in the form of bakground knowledge, which can influence the accuracy of attribute values.

The mechanism can form the basis of designing a user interface to effectively communicate privacy scores and conduct a usability study to understand their effect on the user's privacy awareness.

Based on privacy scores, different types of countermeasures can be suggested to users, taking into account the trade-off between the privacy risks and the social benefits of using OSNs. Such countermeasures include:

- the selection of the right privacy setting for each profile attribute;

- a decision on which friendships to continue based on their effects on the user's privacy scores; and/or

- the negotiation of a privacy setting allowing both the user and his friends to maintain privacy and derive the social benefits of using an OSN.

CHAPTER 7

Social Benefits

In an OSN, a user forms the first impression on other users by revealing different profile attributes such as his age, gender, interests, and workplace. These attributes constitute the basis of building new friendships as well as reviving and enhancing existing ones. Many studies have documented the relationship between the use of OSNs such as Facebook and increased levels of social capital [22, 23, 53–55, 135, 144]. This improvement in the user's social capital, referred to as the *social benefit*, attracts users to OSNs and lures them to reveal a lot of personal data.

This chapter defines the social benefit of OSN profiles and discusses factors that contribute to it and their relationships with user attributes. Next, it discusses a simple method [40] to evaluate the overall social benefit of a user profile based on these factors and relationships.

7.1 · SOCIAL TIES

Haythornthwaite [70] discusses the meaning of ties and their strengths in the context of social networks. A social tie is said to exist among a pair of individuals when they exchange or share resources such as goods, services, social support, or information.

The strength of a social tie can be assessed by measuring various factors or combinations of factors such as the frequency of contact, the duration of association, the intimacy of the tie, and so on.

Strong ties exhibit a higher level of intimacy, self-disclosure, emotional exchanges, trust, and support as well as multiple iterative interactions [55]. On the other hand, weak ties exhibit lower levels for these measures. Weaker ties can provide useful information and new perspectives but generally do not provide emotional support [66]. Examples of strong ties include friends, close friends, co-workers, and team-mates and that of weak ties include friend of a friend [55], acquaintances, casual contacts, and others in an organization [71].

Latent ties are ones that are technically possible, for example, due to the availability of some media of exchange or communication, but are not yet socially activated [71].

Below, we define *on-OSN* and *off-OSN* friends with respect to strong and weak ties.

Definition 7.1 An **off-OSN friend (or tie)** of a target user is an individual with a strong or a weak social tie with the target user and who is connected to the target user via some media (electronic or otherwise) except the online social network under consideration.

Definition 7.2   An **on-OSN friend (or tie)** of a target user is an individual with a strong or a weak social tie with the target user and who is connected to the target user via the online social network (apart from other media) under consideration.

An off-OSN friendship is converted to an on-OSN friendship when the user and his friend establishes a connection via the online social network under consideration.

Off-OSN and on-OSN ties may exhibit different levels of strength. A latent tie can be converted into an on-OSN tie or friendship when the user and the other individual involved in the latent tie establish a connection via the OSN under consideration.

7.2   SOCIAL CAPITAL

The notion of social capital can be understood as capital, similar to human or financial capital, embedded in the relationship between individuals. It refers to the benefits derived by individuals from their social relationships and interactions with their social ties. These benefits may be monetary or non-monetary and include resources such as emotional support, exposure to diverse ideas and access to new and valuable information, better social status, and happiness [54, 55, 115]. Important benefits such as employment connections may result from one's access to individuals outside his or her close social circle [67]. Studies have shown that various types of social capitals, including ties with friends and neighbors, lead to psychological well-being, such as better self esteem and satisfaction with life [12, 73].

Social capital has been described to be an "*elastic term*" having a variety of definitions [4, 53]. According to Lin [94], social capital can be defined as:

"*investment in social relations with expected returns in the marketplace.*"

Social capital, as defined by Bourdieu and Wacquant [20], is

"*the sum of the resources, actual or virtual, that accrue to an individual or a group by virtue of possessing a durable network of more or less institutionalized relationships of mutual acquaintance and recognition.*"

Social capital is often categorized into two types, *bridging* and *bonding* [119, 152], describing resources embedded in different types of relationships [55]. Ties, generally weaker ones, connecting different clusters within a network and thus helping to propagate new information across these groups are referred to as *bridging ties*. Stronger ties, on the other hand, can provide access to bonding social capital such as a financial loan [55].

7.3   UNDERSTANDING SOCIAL BENEFITS

The *social benefit* of a target user from the revealed OSN profile attributes can be defined as [40] follows.

Definition 7.3   The **social benefit** of a target user's profile in an OSN is the overall social capital attained by the target user given the attributes he reveals.

An improvement in social benefits can occur due to a number of factors such as an increase in the number of social ties (for example, through conversion of latent ties to weak ties) and through maintaining and intensifying existing social ties, both of which are possible through OSNs. They can, in turn, be achieved through the disclosure of information which, in the case of OSN profiles, are the user attributes.

Krasnova et al. [88] discuss four perceived benefits of online information disclosure:

- convenience of maintaining relationships,

- relationship building,

- self-presentation, and

- enjoyment.

A study conducted among college students [53] shows that Facebook appears to play an important role in forming and maintaining social capital. An important function of Facebook is to connect users to those they already know in person and also to those they do not know in person [160]. Moreover, it has also been shown that Facebook identities tend to highly emphasize socially desirable characteristics that individuals aspire to have offline [160]. Users also claim to reveal information about themselves that they feel proud about [88].

In the setting of online dating, Ellison et al. [52] discuss the importance of self-presentation strategies during the initiation of relationships as the information is used to decide whether the relationship may be pursued or not. Self-disclosure allows individuals to make themselves known to others and reduce uncertainties and in most cases, have been found to positively affect relationship development [61].

7.3.1   SOCIAL BENEFIT CRITERIA

Different users may have different aims, referred to as *social benefit criteria*, behind owning an OSN profile. While some user may look for new friendships, others may want to get in touch with old off-OSN friends. Formally, social benefit criteria can be defined as follows [40].

Definition 7.4   A **social benefit criteria** of a target user represents the aim of the user behind revealing one or more attributes in his OSN profile toward improving his social capital.

The following are some major social benefit criteria found from user surveys [53, 61, 88, 90, 114, 136]:

- getting in contact with off-OSN friends (SB.1),

- maintaining and intensifying existing on-OSN friendships (SB.2),

- establishing new friendships from common on-OSN circles (SB.3), and

- establishing new friendships outside common on-OSN circle (SB.4).

The rest of this section describes these four criteria.

Getting in Contact with Off-OSN Friends

One of the primary reasons for the use of OSNs is to convert already existing off-OSN strong and weak ties to on-OSN ties. A study by Ellison et al. [53] showed that participants (college students) overwhelmingly used Facebook to keep in touch with old friends and to maintain or intensify friendships characterized by offline connections such as shared classes.

In the same study, it was also evident that: (1) the most commonly revealed information on the user profiles were the ones that would enable existing offline friends to find them (for example, high school); (2) almost all users felt that their high school friends had viewed their profile; and (3) the respondents themselves reported connecting with offline friends as a type of use, as opposed to meeting new people.

Subsequent studies [114, 136] re-iterate that young adults, especially university students, extensively use OSNs to keep in touch with their friends who they meet frequently, old friends who they hardly get a chance to meet regularly, peers, acquaintances, and family members.

Thus, it may be considered that users would, in general, like to establish and stay in touch via the OSN under consideration with not only offline friends but also friends with whom they have a connection via any other media.

Maintaining and Intensifying Existing On-OSN Friendships

Maintenance and intensification of existing on-OSN social ties is another aim that users may have. OSNs are considered to be ideal platforms for quick interactions with many others for the purpose of maintaining relationships, while involving low transaction costs [12, 13, 51, 55, 80, 93, 127, 139, 141–143, 153].

Revealing attributes whose values create a positive impression about oneself as well as those that may help the on-OSN friends to discover more common ground (apart from already known ones) with the user can both lead to increased interaction with these friends and hence enable the maintenance and the intensification of these friendships.

For example, in his workplace, an employee can withhold a lot of information about himself, such as his hobbies, interests, and political views but when connected via an OSN, his colleagues may discover these information about him [75]. The initial connection may have been based only on the fact that they share a workplace, but later the friendship may be intensified due to newly discovered common interests, hobbies, and political opinion or positive impression. For example, one respondent in a related study [75] said that they found out that their co-worker is a wonderful baker.

In addition, Krasnova et al. [88] discuss that the ease of maintenance of friendships through OSNs due to the reduced requirement of time investment (all friends are "one-click away" [88]) and the increased possibilities of reciprocity motivate users to reveal personal information on OSN.

Establishing New Friendships from Common On-OSN Circles

Establishing new friendships from common on-OSN circles comprises the conversion of latent ties among on-OSN friends-of-friends to weak ties.

There may exist several other users of the OSN in the target user's friends-of-friends circle who may share some common grounds with the user, but who are neither off-OSN nor on-OSN strong or weak ties of the target user. In other words, they are latent ties, who may share the same workplace, education level, or interests as the target user. So, the target user may find it useful to convert such latent ties into weak ties by befriending them via the OSN.

Users can benefit from new contacts by accumulating social capital as the latter may provide more useful information and perspectives [53] as their experiences, information, attitude, resources, and contacts stem from different social spheres [71].

The disclosure of information and the intention to develop new friendships have been shown to be tightly linked [61] and by disclosing specific attributes about oneself, the user sends desired signals that help them to establish contacts with individuals who share a common ground [90]. For example, in the study by Krasnova et al. [88], one respondent said that she reveals information so that people who share her hobbies can contact her.

Establishing New Friendships Outside Common On-OSN Circle

Establishing new friendships outside common on-OSN circle comprise the conversion of latent ties among strangers to weak ties.

There may exist several users of the OSN even outside the target user's friends-of-friends circle who may share some common grounds with the user, but who are neither off-OSN nor on-OSN strong or weak ties of the target user. They are also latent ties, who may have the same workplace, education level or interests as the target user. So, the target user may find it useful to convert such latent ties into weak ties by befriending them via the OSN.

Further Discussions

The foremost reason for differentiating latent ties within and beyond the friends-of-friends circle is that the friends-of-friends circle may tend to share many common grounds (although less compared to friends) with the user and is thus more similar to the user in terms of experience,

Table 7.1: Attribute revelation to achieve social benefit criteria

Code (*SB.i*)	Attributes to be Revealed (*d*)	Desired Level of Revelation (*l*)
SB.1	W.Pl, Edu.Pl	A.3
SB.2	B.Dt, Ph., H.Add, Int, Pol, Rel, RStat	A.1
SB.3	Int, Pol, Rel, W.Pl, Gen, Edu.Pl, RStat, B.Yr	A.2
SB.4	H.City, Int, Pol, Rel, W.Pl, Gen, Edu.Pl, RStat, B.Yr	A.3

contacts and resources, than the strangers beyond the friends-of-friends circle. The latter tend to share far less similarities with the user as they move in different social circles. Therefore, the social benefits derived from a friendship that originates from the friends-of-friends circle and that which originates beyond it may be very different.

The privacy setting of the social network usually differentiates between friends-of-friends and strangers. So when the motivation of the target user is to convert latent ties only in the friends-of-friends circle to weak ties, he should reveal the attributes that may help in this conversion only to his friends-of-friends. However, if he also wants the same for strangers, he must reveal the attributes to strangers too.

Different user groups such as young adults and teens may give different levels of importance to these social benefit criteria. Studies show that compared to young adults who use Facebook mostly to remain in touch with their offline friends, acquaintances and family members, teenagers assign more importance to making new friends through OSNs [114].

7.3.2   ATTRIBUTES AND SOCIAL BENEFIT CRITERIA

Each social benefit criteria can be achieved by revealing certain attributes to certain users of the OSN. Table 7.1 lists attributes that can help achieve the four social benefit criteria discussed above, based on related literature [53, 90].

For example, users who share their workplaces (W.Pl) can refer to shared traditions and locations establishing the common ground necessary to reconnect with off-OSN friends and to build new on-OSN friendships. Revealing one's home address or phone number to on-OSN friends can indicate willingness to be contacted even outside the OSN [90], showing a desire to intensify existing on-OSN friendships.

Each user attribute contributes to one or more social benefit criteria. For example, the birth date (B.Dt) of the target user only contributes to *SB*.2 and no other criteria. Interests (Int) of the target user contributes to *SB*.2, *SB*.3, and *SB*.4.

Each attribute must have a desired privacy setting in order to satisfy the criteria it corresponds to. For example, all attributes for *SB*.4 must have the privacy setting of {A.1,A.2,A.3} whereas all attributes for *SB*.2 must have the privacy setting of {A.1}. Thus, Table 7.1 also presents the desired privacy settings corresponding to each attribute in order to achieve each social benefit criteria.

7.4   EVALUATION OF SOCIAL BENEFIT

How can the overall social benefit of an OSN user profile be evaluated? Revealing certain attributes and hiding others, i.e., the decision $\mathbf{x}$, affect user's overall social benefit. This overall social benefit can be computed using the function[1]:

$$SB(\mathbf{x}) : X \rightarrow \mathbb{Z}^+ \cup \{0\}. \qquad (7.1)$$

This section describes one simple method [40] for this evaluation.

As discussed in the previous section, each attribute, revealed at a desired level, helps to achieve one or more social benefit criteria. The contribution or weight $w_{d,l,i}$ of attribute d when revealed at level l (e.g., friends, friends-of-friends or public) to achieve a social benefit criteria $SB.i$ (where $i = 1, \ldots, n$) depends on individual target users. Here, the focus remains on the four social benefit criteria described in Section 7.3.1. In general, other social benefit criteria could also be used.

For a target user who uses an OSN mainly for the purpose of connecting to off-OSN friends ($SB.1$), publishing his place of work (W.Pl) to all users of the OSN ($A.3$) is more important than publishing his birthday (B.Dt) or place of work (W.Pl) only to his on-OSN friends ($A.1$). Similarly, for a target user who wants to establish new friendships only from common on-OSN circle ($SB.3$), revealing his interests (Int), workplace (W.Pl), etc. to his friends-of-friends ($A.2$) is sufficient (compared to revealing the same to all users of the OSN, i.e., $A.3$). Thus, each target user must assign a score, denoted by $w_{SB.i}$, to each social benefit criteria to describe whether that criteria is important (score 1) or not important (score 0) to him.

Then, it is assumed that this score assigned by the user to a social benefit criteria exactly reflects the contributions of the attributes to that criteria. So, the weight $w_{d,l,i}$, i.e., the contribution of an attribute d revealed at level l toward the social benefit criteria $SB.i$ is the same as the score $w_{SB.i}$ assigned by the user to the social benefit criteria $SB.i$. That is,

$$w_{d,l,i} = w_{SB.i}. \qquad (7.2)$$

Note that each social benefit criteria involves a set of attributes as indicated in Table 7.1. Then, the total weight $w_{d,l}$ of the attribute d when revealed at level l is given by:

$$w_{d,l} = \sum_i w_{d,l,i}. \qquad (7.3)$$

---

[1]The range of $SB(.)$ can also be $\mathbb{R}^+ \cup \{0\}$ depending on how this function is defined.

Not all combinations of d, l, and i in $w_{d,l,i}$ are valid. Only the valid combinations are presented in Table 7.1. For example, B.Dt, $SB.2$, and $A.1$ is a valid combination but B.Dt, $SB.4$, and $A.1$ is not. For invalid combinations of d, l, and i, one can consider that:

$$w_{d,l,i} = 0. \tag{7.4}$$

Suppose the user has assigned the following scores to the different social benefit criteria:

$$w_{SB.1} = w_{SB.4} = 1 \tag{7.5}$$

$$w_{SB.2} = w_{SB.3} = 0. \tag{7.6}$$

Then, we can obtain:

$$w_{W.Pl,A.3,1} = w_{W.Pl,A.3,4} = 1. \tag{7.7}$$

Since $w_{W.Pl,A.3,2} = w_{W.Pl,A.3,3} = 0$ as the corresponding d, l, and i are invalid combinations,

$$w_{W.Pl,A.3} = \sum_i w_{W.Pl,A.3,i} = w_{W.Pl,A.3,1} + w_{W.Pl,A.3,2} + w_{W.Pl,A.3,3} + w_{W.Pl,A.3,4} = 2. \tag{7.8}$$

The overall social benefit of user's profile is given by:

$$SB(\mathbf{x}) = \sum_{d,l} w_{d,l} \cdot x_{d,l}, \tag{7.9}$$

where $\mathbf{x} = (x_{d,l})$ and $x_{d,l}$ represents whether an attribute d at level l has been revealed or not (i.e., $x_{d,l} \in \{0, 1\}$).

7.5   OPEN PROBLEMS

This chapter has provided a preliminary overview of social benefits and how the overall social benefit of an OSN profile can be computed. Below are some important directions for further exploration in this area.

So far, only a few important social benefit criteria have been considered. Many other criteria may exist, especially for different types of OSNs. For example, the motivations for using LinkedIn may be different from that for Facebook. Similarly, the motivations for using Twitter may be different from that of Facebook or LinkedIn. So, there is a scope to study existing surveys or perform new surveys on why users participate in these different types of OSNs and add more social benefit criteria to the list already mentioned in the chapter and link these with contributing attributes.

The social benefits derived by different types of users may be different. For example, a business entity may derive monetary benefits by attracting new friends and followers in OSNs whereas a college student may use the OSN to keep in touch with her high school friends. A study of such variations across user groups is another worthwhile direction to explore.

In general, attributes may not contribute equally to all the social benefit criteria they cater to. For example, the attribute Int contributes differently to $SB.2$ than it does to $SB.3$ or $SB.4$. Even for a given social benefit criteria, the contribution of the different attributes may not be the same. For example, more off-OSN friends may be able to contact a target user if he mentions his places of education (Edu.Pl) compared to the cities he has lived in (H.City). These levels of contributions may be taken into account in the evaluation of social benefits.

In the social benefit evaluation mechanism described in this chapter, the user has to provide inputs on whether a social benefit criteria is important or not by assigning a score of 1 or 0, respectively. More levels of scoring may be included, for example, to denote whether a social benefit criteria is very important, important, or not important at all. It may also be possible to eliminate the requirement for user intervention at this stage by automatically inferring what social benefit criteria is important to a user based on his past attribute revelation habits.

The social benefits derived from attribute revelation have been described in the current discourse. The social benefits derived specifically from the dynamic part of the user profile such as posts, comments and likes could be explored further. The action of liking a friend's post may be considered helpful in maintaining or intensifying the existing relationship. Similarly, the effect of positive and negative comments on a friend's post may serve different purposes and need to be studied in detail. For example, writing a comment in support of the opinion expressed in a friend's post may intensify the friendship; on the other hand, writing an opposing viewpoint in the comment may negatively affect the friendship.

CHAPTER 8

Choosing the Right Privacy Settings

Privacy settings in OSN profiles allow users to choose the level of visibility of the attributes they reveal. When chosen correctly, the privacy settings of an attribute restricts the data to the intended audience. In Facebook for example, the user can keep an attribute private or reveal it to his friends or friends-of-friends or make it public. So, a user may keep his phone number private, reveal his birth date to his friends, his work place to his friends-of-friends and interests to all users of the OSN.

Ideally, the user must consider a number of factors if he wants to choose the *right* privacy settings.

First, he must keep in mind the social benefits he wants to gain by revealing an attribute. So, if his main interest is to re-establish contact with his old high school friends via the OSN, he should reveal his high school to the public.

Second, to protect his privacy, the user must consider the privacy harms an attribute may cause alone or in combination with other attributes. An OSN profile consists of several attributes and most users do not fully understand how the revelation of different attribute combinations can lead to these harms.

Third, the attributes revealed by his friends may be used to infer the user's own attributes. Such inferences cannot be prevented using the user's own privacy settings and he must be willing to tolerate a residual risk even after he makes the *right* choice. Moreover, these inferences influence which attributes the user should reveal and hence, also the social benefits that he can gain.

Fourth, given some specific social benefit preferences, the user cannot be protected against all privacy harms.

Since so many factors are involved in the decision making, choosing the right privacy setting is a complicated task for the user. In most cases, without additional support system, this may cause users to either not reveal any information out of privacy concerns, thus damaging the sustainability of OSNs [87] or reveal more information than they prefer [103] increasing their vulnerability.

The EU General Data Protection Regulation (GDPR) [56] emphasizes on data subjects' control over personal data and that they should be made aware of the risks related to personal data processing. For example, Recital 7 states that:

> "*Natural persons should have control of their own personal data*",

while Recital 39 states that:

> "*Natural persons should be made aware of risks, rules, safeguards and rights in relation to the processing of personal data and how to exercise their rights in relation to such processing.*"

While privacy scores make users aware of risks, providing users with additional support to choose the right privacy settings based on a clear appraisal of risks and benefits, enhances their control over their personal data.

This chapter first provides a brief overview of privacy management models that take into account the privacy and social benefit tradeoff in OSNs. Among these models, the chapter describes a two-phase, Integer Programming-based approach to privacy setting management [40]. This approach, for the first time, has encouraged users to protect their privacy as much as possible, while maximizing their social benefits at the same time, using privacy risk analysis concepts and an optimization model.

8.1   PRIVACY AND SOCIAL BENEFIT TRADEOFF IN PRIVACY MANAGEMENT

Users are made aware of the privacy risks of their information sharing actions on OSNs through privacy scores. But what should users do to manage their privacy risks in OSNs? More particularly, how should users choose their friends, or choose the privacy settings of the information they share in order to minimize this risk? And, how could they take into account the benefits of OSN use while protecting themselves from privacy risks?

Today, there is an increasing interest [17, 18, 28, 29, 40, 42, 69, 81, 109, 110, 113, 120, 121, 158] in considering the trade-off between the social benefits of information sharing and privacy concerns in OSNs to aid users in privacy management. Different types of models, such as machine learning based [17, 18, 120, 121], game theory based [16, 28, 29, 81, 109, 110, 113, 130, 131] and PRA and Integer Programming (IP) based [40, 42], have been used to incorporate this trade-off in privacy management. Below we provide a brief overview of some of these approaches.

Machine Learning based Models

Machine learning based models rely on learning privacy and benefits related factors that influence the user's decision on information sharing [17, 18]. A user may be aided in his choice of the optimal privacy settings based on these by learning the relationship between privacy settings and existing users' latent levels of privacy concerns and implicit utility preferences based on the privacy settings chosen by these existing users [69]. From the viewpoint of dynamic nature of social relationships and the nature of information, the same problem may be addressed by learning how, with time, the nature and strength of relationships between a user and the members of his social groups and the sensitivity of information change [120, 121].

Game-theoretic Models

Game theory helps to analyze scenarios involving conflicts and cooperation among rational decision-makers through mathematical modelling [101, 111]. Rational decision-makers (or players) tend to take decisions that maximize their utility. In OSNs, a number of game theoretic models [28, 29, 81, 113, 130] have been proposed to analyze the users' decisions to reveal or withhold his attributes, the extent to which he reveals (for example, to his friends or friends-of-friends) and the effect of such decisions on other users. These analyses have often shown that users' decision to reveal their attributes are not often strongly guided by concerns about privacy risks [29, 130]. Rather, users tend to reveal those attributes that bring in larger social benefits than others [29] and the amount of information shared also depends on benefits such as gaining and maintaining popularity [130].

Popular OSNs like Facebook and Foursquare enable users to share their location as well as co-location with other users. Sharing of co-location, even without actually revealing the location, has benefits for both the user who is sharing as well as the viewers of this information. Usually, people like to share who they are with and like to know who their friends are with. However, location information generally involves many privacy concerns. For co-location information, the privacy concerns relate to all the users who are involved.

Similarly, while many users (and even non-users) may appear in an image, a user can share it or tag it without having to ask for the consent of the others. In this case also, the level of privacy enjoyed by one is determined by the privacy preferences of the sharing user, in spite of the fact that they may have conflicting privacy preferences.

These situations raise the requirement of collaborative or interdependent privacy management. In this context, a number of game theoretic approaches have been undertaken to model and analyze the benefits and the privacy implications of information sharing and the resulting strategic behaviours of users [16, 109, 110] and to promote fairness [131].

PRA and IP-based Models

The use of privacy risk analysis (PRA) concepts such as privacy harms, harm trees and risk sources to enable users to effectively manage their privacy through assisted privacy setting selection was first introduced in [42]. Their Integer Programming (IP)-based model [42] helps the OSN user choose the optimal privacy settings of his profile attributes, without relying on his own judgement. This optimal settings enables the user to achieve the maximum social benefit while protecting himself from all or at least some major privacy risks.

The optimization problem is formulated as an Integer Programming (IP) problem. Privacy risks are evaluated based on harm trees and social benefits are computed based on existing studies on the benefits of data sharing in OSNs.

This PRA and IP-based model has been expanded into a two-phase approach in [40] taking into account the fact that the inference of personal data from the user's vicinity affects the attributes to be revealed and contributes to a residual risk that the user must tolerate in spite of choosing the right privacy settings. The first phase allows the user to understand which privacy harms he can avoid, after tolerating residual risks, given his social benefit requirements. The second phase provides the user with the privacy settings for his attributes to gain the maximum social benefit from his OSN profile.

8.2   AN INTEGER PROGRAMMING MODEL

Integer Programming [74] (IP) problems are a special form of the Linear Programming (LP) problem. An LP problem consists of *decision variables* representing unknown decisions or quantities to be optimized. The aim is to *maximize* or *minimize* the value of an *objective function*, a linear function of the decision variables, subject to certain requirements and restrictions, referred to as *constraints*.

Each constraint requires that a linear function of the decision variables is either equal to, not more than or not less than a scalar value. IP problems have the additional restriction that some of the decision variables must take on integer values.

An IP problem may have one or multiple optimal solutions or no feasible solution. One can find out whether a solution exists and if so, the value of the objective function by finding out any one optimal solution. It is also possible to find out alternate optimal solutions. However, enumerating all optimal solutions may be more difficult than solving the optimization problem itself [76].

Optimization through the use of Integer Programming has also been used in other areas of security and privacy [19, 82].

8.2.1   BALANCING PRIVACY RISKS AND SOCIAL BENEFITS

Mathematically speaking, the right privacy setting for a user consists of the values of the decision variables $\mathbf{x}$ such that the corresponding social benefit $SB(\mathbf{x})$ is maximum and at the same time certain constraints are satisfied, i.e., certain privacy risks are avoided. Such an $\mathbf{x}$ is referred to as the *optimal solution*.

The primary set of constraints is that the privacy risks $R_i(\mathbf{x})$ should be within the risk tolerance thresholds t_i for all harms h_i, i.e., $R_i(\mathbf{x}) \leq t_i, i = 1, \ldots, n$. The notations used henceforth have been described in Chapter 2.

In addition, some other constraints related to the social benefits, privacy settings and the nature of the decision variables (binary or otherwise) must be satisfied.

A simple, high level view of the optimization problem (only with the primary constraints, for simplicity) as an Integer Programming model is as follows:

$$\begin{array}{ll} \text{Maximize} & SB(\mathbf{x}) \\ \text{subject to} & R_i(\mathbf{x}) \le t_i, \quad i = 1, \dots, n \\ & \mathbf{x} \in X \end{array} \qquad (8.1)$$

The user can use the optimal solution of the above optimization problem to choose the appropriate privacy settings for each of his profile attributes.

The challenge is to appropriately construct:

- the objective function, i.e., the function $SB(.)$ and

- the primary constraints related to privacy risks, i.e., the functions $R_i(.)$.

Methods of computing the privacy risks and social benefits from a user's OSN profile have already been described in Chapter 6 and Chapter 7 respectively.

Other necessary constraints related to social benefits and the privacy settings must also be formulated.

One must keep in mind that, given a user's social benefit requirements, his OSN profile cannot be protected from all privacy harms always, due to the trade-off between privacy risk and social benefits of attribute revelation. Moreover, since the attributes revealed by the user's vicinity can be used to reveal those of the user and privacy settings cannot be used to prevent such inference, a residual risk may always exist [161] even if the user does not reveal the attributes contributing to the harm(s). The computation of residual risks has been discussed in Chapter 6.

The IP model only concerns those attributes that contribute to harm(s) as well as social benefit(s). The same attribute (d) revealed at different levels (l) may or may not contribute to both harm(s) and social benefit(s). For example, phone number may be harmful when revealed to strangers, but when revealed to only friends, it may be beneficial. Attributes that only contribute to social benefit(s) must always be revealed by the user. Attributes that only contribute to a harm must always be hidden.

In general, a user is aware of what social benefits he would like to gather from an OSN but is not sure about what privacy harms he can avoid while fulfilling these requirements. As an input, he must specify his social benefit requirements by assigning some scores to the social benefit criteria as discussed in Chapter 7. These scores are necessary for evaluating $SB(\mathbf{x})$ and the formulation of the social benefit constraints.

Although a user may be privacy concerned [87, 103] and thus has some idea about the consequences of privacy risks, he is not a privacy expert and hence has limited knowledge about how the revelation of different personal data may lead to different privacy harms. Therefore, he requires help to determine the risk tolerance thresholds (t_i) that is appropriate to achieve his social benefit requirements.

The output of the first phase is the most privacy-preserving threshold combination that will help the user to achieve the best overall social benefit, given his social benefit scores. Given this threshold combination and the user's social benefit scores, the second phase provides the privacy settings that the user must choose to maximize his social benefits.

8.3   FORMULATION OF THE IP PROBLEM

The IP problem that forms the crux of the two-phase approach[1] consists of an objective function and three types of constraints. The first type of constraint restricts the privacy risks. Each of these constraints ensures that the risk evaluated for a harm using a harm tree is less than the risk tolerance threshold, t_i, for that particular harm. The second type of constraints presents the restrictions originating from the social benefit criteria. The third type of constraints helps to enforce the restrictions due to the privacy settings. Additional constraints are used to specify that some decision variables are binary, while others belong to the interval $[0, 1]$.

8.3.1   OBJECTIVE FUNCTION

The overall social benefit of the user's profile is:

$$SB(\mathbf{x}) = \sum_{d,l} w_{d,l}.x_{d,l} \tag{8.2}$$

where $\mathbf{x} = (x_{d,l})$ and $x_{d,l}$ represents the decision to reveal attribute d at level l. The aim is to maximize this social benefit, so the above expression is used as the objective function of the IP problem 8.1.

8.3.2   PRIVACY RISK CONSTRAINTS

The constraints that restrict the privacy risks in the IP model 8.1 can be obtained from the harm expressions defined in terms of the max and the min functions.

The constraints for the harms h_1 and h_3 are given by the inequalities 8.3 and 8.4 respectively. The risk tolerance threshold $t_i \in \{a_i, 1\}$ (where $0 \leq a_i < 1$) required for the ith harm denotes whether:

- the profile is to be protected from the harm h_i to the extent allowed by the vicinity ($t_i = a_i$), or

- the harm h_i is simply tolerated ($t_i = 1$).

$$min(max(y_{B.Yr,A.3}, y_{Gen,A.3}), max(y_{W.Pl,A.3}, y_{H.Add,A.3})) \leq t_1 \tag{8.3}$$
$$min(y_{B.Dt,A.3}, y_{B.Yr,A.3}, y_{H.Add,A.3}, y_{Ph.,A.3}) \leq t_3 \tag{8.4}$$

[1]More details on algorithms for the two-phase method can be found in [40].

Table 8.1: An example of a set of social benefit constraints

Importance Assigned by Target User	Social Benefit Constraints
$SB.1$ is not important	$x_{W.Pl,A.3} = 0$
$SB.1$ is important	$x_{W.Pl,A.3} \geq 0$
$SB.2$ is not important	$x_{B.Dt,A.1} + x_{Ph.,A.1} + x_{H.Add,A.1} + x_{Int,A.1} + x_{Pol,A.1} + x_{Rel,A.1} + x_{RStat,A.1} \leq 3$
$SB.2$ is important	$x_{B.Dt,A.1} + x_{Ph.,A.1} + x_{H.Add,A.1} + x_{Int,A.1} + x_{Pol,A.1} + x_{Rel,A.1} + x_{RStat,A.1} \geq 4$
$SB.3$ is not important	$x_{B.Yr,A.2} + x_{W.Pl,A.2} + x_{Gen,A.2} + x_{Int,A.2} + x_{Pol,A.2} + x_{Rel,A.2} + x_{RStat,A.2} \leq 3$
$SB.3$ is important	$x_{B.Yr,A.2} + x_{W.Pl,A.2} + x_{Gen,A.2} + x_{Int,A.2} + x_{Pol,A.2} + x_{Rel,A.2} + x_{RStat,A.2} \geq 4$
$SB.4$ is not important	$x_{B.Yr,A.3} + x_{W.Pl,A.3} + x_{Gen,A.3} + x_{Int,A.3} + x_{Pol,A.3} + x_{Rel,A.3} + x_{RStat,A.3} = 0$
$SB.4$ is important	$x_{B.Yr,A.3} + x_{W.Pl,A.3} + x_{Gen,A.3} + x_{Int,A.3} + x_{Pol,A.3} + x_{Rel,A.3} + x_{RStat,A.3} \geq 0$

However, both these inequalities are non-linear in nature and need to be linearized for the IP model.

In the IP model, the decision variables $x_{d,l}$ are binary, whereas, the decision variable $y_{d,l}$ can assume values in the interval $[0, 1]$.

8.3.3   SOCIAL BENEFIT CONSTRAINTS

The general idea behind the construction of the social benefit constraints is that the number and the type of attributes revealed must reflect the level of importance of different social benefits to a user and the harms these attributes lead to. An example of a set of social benefit constraints is presented in Table 8.1.

Whereas some attributes revealed at a particular level contribute to harm(s) as well as bring in some social benefit, others only contribute to the latter. While constructing these constraints, one must therefore keep in mind that revelation of attributes that contribute to both harms and benefits are already being considered for restriction by privacy risk constraints. Further restrictions on their revelation may render the model infeasible under many scenarios.

If the user finds a particular social benefit to be important and only some of the corresponding attributes lead to harm, then the majority of these attributes should be revealed. Otherwise, less than half the attributes should be revealed when this same social benefit is perceived as unimportant.

On the other hand, if a social benefit where all attributes also contribute to one or more harms, is important to the user, then some of these attributes may be revealed. Conversely, none of the attributes should be revealed when such a social benefit is unimportant.

8.3.4 PRIVACY SETTING CONSTRAINTS

Generally, an attribute revealed to strangers (A.3) is also visible to friends (A.1) and friends-of-friends (A.2) and an attribute revealed to friends-of-friends is also visible to friends (A.2).

In addition, if an attribute is not revealed at all, it is private. So, given this nature of the privacy settings, for all attributes d in D, the following constraints must be satisfied:

$$x_{d,A.2} - x_{d,A.3} \geq 0 \tag{8.5}$$
$$x_{d,A.1} - x_{d,A.2} \geq 0 \tag{8.6}$$
$$x_{d,A.1} + x_{d,A.2} + x_{d,A.3} \geq 0 \tag{8.7}$$

Constraint 8.5 ensures that whenever an attribute is revealed to A.3 (i.e., $x_{d,A.3} = 1$), it is revealed to A.2 as well (i.e., $x_{d,A.2} = x_{d,A.3} = 1$). However, if it is not revealed to A.3 (i.e., $x_{d,A.3} = 0$), then it may or may not be revealed to A.2 (i.e., $x_{d,A.2} = x_{d,A.3} = 0$ or $x_{d,A.2} = 1$ which means $x_{d,A.2} > x_{d,A.3}$).

Similarly, Constraint 8.6 ensures that whenever an attribute is revealed to A.2, it is revealed to A.1 as well, but if it is not revealed to A.2, then it may or may not be revealed to A.1.

Constraint 8.7 ensures that an attribute may be revealed to some or all users ($A.1$, $A.2$ and/or $A.3$) (i.e., $x_{d,A.1} + x_{d,A.2} + x_{d,A.3} > 0$) or may be kept private (i.e., $x_{d,A.1} + x_{d,A.2} + x_{d,A.3} = 0$).

8.4 OPEN PROBLEMS

The IP-model based two-phase approach described in this chapter assists a user to select an appropriate privacy settings for his profile attributes to maximize his social benefits. It also helps him to understand the privacy harms that can be avoided, after tolerating residual risks, given his social benefit requirements.

The accuracy of attribute inference from the user's vicinity influences the attributes to be revealed and hence the social benefits of the user. So this approach can be used to help the user to find ways to alter his vicinity. One can identify which friends are risky and contribute to the inference of a large number of attribute values. They can also evaluate the social benefits derived from these friends. While removing a risky friend is beneficial from the privacy perspective, it may not be helpful from the social benefits perspective. So, once such friends are identified, different types of countermeasures should be considered. A risky friend who does not contribute to many social benefits may be entirely removed from the friend list or put in a separate group. Users can then benefit from privacy settings that allows sharing with all friends except some specific ones, by excluding these risky-but-not-beneficial friends from all sharing activities. Similarly, friends who are risky but also significantly contribute to many social benefits may be alerted to improve their privacy settings.

Further, the model can be extended to suggest the privacy settings of dynamic data (for a given time period) in OSN profiles, such as posts and comments, by extracting personal data revealed by them [5] through automated text analysis, for better privacy protection. It can also be adapted for the privacy settings of specific OSNs.

CHAPTER 9

Conclusion

The privacy scoring and privacy settings management mechanisms described in this discourse are early attempts to introduce privacy risk analysis concepts in the area of online social networks (OSNs) from the user perspective. They are also in alignment with the risk-based approach of the EU GDPR toward privacy protection. Privacy scores make users aware of their privacy risks and privacy management support helps user with the complex decision of choosing the right privacy settings for their OSN profiles. Therefore, risk awareness and control over one's personal data are achieved through these mechanisms.

The intersection of OSNs and privacy risk analysis (PRA) from a user's perspective have many open problems that deserve attention from researchers. A lot of these open problems have already been discussed at the end of relevant chapters as they are quite specific in nature. However, more general problems exist and await to be explored. Some of these are discussed below.

Over the years many privacy scoring mechanisms have been proposed. For a naive user it then becomes a highly complicated task to select which privacy scoring mechanism should be used to get the best results. Therefore, there exists a scope for the development of a privacy impact assessment-(PIA) based standard for user privacy protection in OSNs.

In general, PRA and broadly PIA are meant for data controllers to understand the privacy risks of their services for data subjects. Although use-case-specific PIA and PRA have been proposed, for example, for RFID-based and location-based systems, no such in-depth proposal exists for OSNs even though the latter raise numerous privacy concerns. Similarly, PRA or PIA-based mechanisms to help users assess their privacy risks are scarce till date. Not only in the context of OSNs, but also for other applications, such mechanisms can help users to make complex privacy-related decisions much more wisely, without much hassles thus empowering them with the control over their own personal data.

Another important area that deserves more PRA-based mechanisms is collaborative privacy management. Although friends may pose several privacy risks by revealing what a user does not want to reveal, they also bring in several social benefits. Therefore, careful negotiation with friends on the privacy settings of data that have multiple stakeholders keeping in mind both privacy risks and social benefits is necessary. This is an area where PRA-based mechanisms could make significant contributions, for example, by building harm trees that can convince multiple parties on why such negotiations are important. In addition, PRA-based friendship management solutions can be proposed to accept friend requests based on a careful weighing of the privacy risks and social benefits brought about by the potential new connection. Similarly, existing friends can be grouped into categories signifying their risk levels and offered benefits. Information can then be shared based on these categorizations.

APPENDIX A

Notations and Their Meanings

Table A.1: List of notations and their meanings (*Continues*)

Notation	Meaning
T	Target user
$\mathbb{A}_d$	Set of attributes
d	An attribute in $\mathbb{A}_d$
d_{v_i}	ith value of attribute d
$A.k$	kth risk source, $k = 1, 2, 3$
h_i	ith harm
$FE.i$	ith threat
$P_{R,T}$	Real profile of target user T
$P_{V,T,k}$	Virtual profile of target user T as observed by risk source $A.k$
d_{true}	True value of attribute d as presented in real profile $P_{R,T}$
$\mathbb{T}$	Set of friends of the target user
$Acc(A.k, d)$	Accuracy of attribute d for risk source $A.k$, $k = 1, 2, 3$
$Acc_r(A.k, d)$	Real accuracy of attribute d for risk source $A.k$, $k = 1, 2, 3$
$\mathbb{M}$	Visibility matrix
$\mathbb{M}[T,d]$	Visibility of attribute d as set by the target user T
$\mathbb{M}[T_1,d]$	Visibility of attribute d as set by the target user's friend T_1
$Vis_{true}[T,d]$	True visibility of target user Ts attribute d
T'	Dummy user who is a friend of T
T''	Dummy user who is a friend of T' and hence a friend of friend of T
SB_i	ith social benefit criteria
L_d	Set of levels of revelation

Table A.1: (*Continued*) List of notations and their meanings

$x_{d,l}$	Decision whether the attribute d is to be revealed at level l
$w_{d,l,i}$	The contribution of an attribute d revealed at level l toward the social benefit criteria $SB.i$
$w_{SB.i}$	Score assigned by the user to the social benefit criteria $SB.i$
$SB(\mathbf{x})$	Overall social benefit of user's profile
$P_{s,k}$	Profile similarity with respect to risk source $A.k$

APPENDIX B

Comparison of Privacy Scoring Mechanisms

Table B.1: A comparison of privacy scoring mechanisms ("−": dimension is unspecified; "×": dimension is irrelevant) (*Continues*)

Privacy Scoring Mechanisms	Type of Data	Privacy Setting	Assumption about User	Inference Method	Privacy Scores
Privometer [138]	Attributes	Malicious app installed in friends' profiles	−	Method that infers an attribute most accurately among a list of inference methods	Combined probability of inferring all sensitive attributes
PrivAware [16]	Attributes	Third-party applications	−	Most popular (exceeding a threshold) value in the vicinity	Percentage of attributes revealed
Privacy disclosure score [5]	Static, dynamic data	Polytomous	−	×	Privacy score for the overall profile
Privacy risk score [9, 10]	Dynamic data	Multiple levels of friendship	×	×	Privacy risk of each message
Latent trait theory-based model [96]	Attributes	Dichotomous, polytomous	If a user hides an attribute, it is sensitive	×	Privacy score of the user profile
PIDX [151]	Attributes	Polytomous	−	−	Overall privacy index based on all known attributes

Table B.1: (*Continued*) A comparison of privacy scoring mechanisms ("−": dimension is unspecified; "×": dimension is irrelevant)

PScore [118]	Static and dynamic data	Polytomous	Privacy concerns vary across users and hence each user's personal preference must be considered	Possibility to use multiple inference mechanisms	Privacy scores at the level of attribute values, attributes, privacy dimensions, and overall
PRA-based model [40]	Attributes	Polytomous	Users are aware of consequences of privacy harms, but not how different attribute combinations lead to harms	Most popular value among the target user's immediate friends	Likelihood for each harm, profile similarity for the profile

APPENDIX C

Cases 3 and 4

This appendix describes Case 3 and Case 4 in the process of populating the visibility matrix with the help of Figures C.1, C.2, C.3, and C.4. Case 1 and Case 2 of the process was discussed in Chapter 4.

In these figures, each node represents an OSN user. Node T is the target user. Nodes T_1 and T_2 are his friends, Node T_3 is a friend of T_1. Node M_1 is a mutual friend of T and T_1. Similarly, M_3 is a mutual friend of T and T_3. Node N_1 is a non-mutual friend of T_1 and N_3 is a non-mutual friend of T_3. T' and T'' are dummy friend and friend-of-friend of T, respectively, and have been created for the purpose of constructing the visibility matrix of the target user T.

In the figures, all real friendship links are depicted by solid lines between the nodes. Dummy friendship links (i.e., ones created artificially) are depicted by dotted lines between the nodes.

Below are the descriptions of Case 3 and Case 4.

Case 3. An attribute d of a friend T_1 is visible from T and T' but not from T''. In this case, the privacy setting used by T_1 for d is "friends-of-friends." Now, the corresponding cell in the visibility matrix with the risk sources who can view T_1's attribute d from the point of view of T must be filled. To do this, first the visibility is collected by repeating the process when the attribute d is only visible to T (i.e., the process outlined under Case 2). Next, if the visibility set thus derived contains the risk source $A.2$ and T_1 has a public friendlist, then for all friends of T_1, one again checks the visibility and adds new risk sources, if any. The presence of $A.2$ in the visibility set when T_1's friendlist is public implies that there is at least one non-mutual friend of T_1. Now, the visibility of the attribute due to the friends of this non-mutual friend of T_1 must be checked.

Scenario 1: Public Friendlist. If the friendlist of the non-mutual friend of T_1 is public, then the existence of mutual and non-mutual friends of T_1 with the target user T is checked. Additionally, whether T itself has a non-mutual friend (e.g., T_2) is checked and if so, whether this friend also has a non-mutual friend (if its friendlist is public). Then, the following cases arise.

3.1.a. Only Mutual Friends. There are only mutual friend(s) between T_3 and T other than T_1 and T has no non-mutual friend. In other words, all friends of T_3 are also friends of T. In this case, the attribute is visible to the risk sources $A.1$ and $A.2$ (i.e., to the friends of T including the mutual friends of T_3 and T and T_3 itself) from

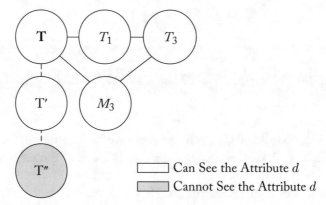

Figure C.1: Attribute visibility when T_1's privacy setting is "friends-of-friends" and T_3 has only a mutual friend M_3.

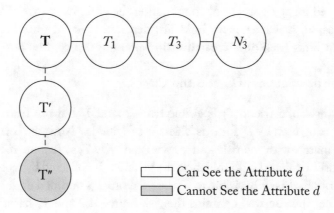

Figure C.2: Attribute visibility when T_1's privacy setting is "friends-of-friends" and T_3 only has non-mutual friend N_3.

T's perspective and so the visibility set is assigned the value $\{A.1, A.2\}$. Figure C.1 depicts this scenario. The visibility set is assigned the value $\{A.1, A.2\}$ even when T has non-mutual friend(s), other conditions remaining the same. If this non-mutual friend of T again has non-mutual friend(s) (only when it has public friendlist), other conditions remaining the same, then Vis is assigned the value $\{A.1, A.2, A.3\}$.

3.1.b. Only Non-Mutual Friends. There is no mutual friend between T_3 and T except T_1 but T_3 has non-mutual friend(s) and T does not have a non-mutual friend. In other words, no friend of T_3 is a friend of T. In this case, the attribute is visible to the risk sources $A.2$ and $A.3$ (i.e., to the non-mutual friends of T_3 who are strangers with respect to T and T_3 itself) from T's perspective and so Vis is assigned the value

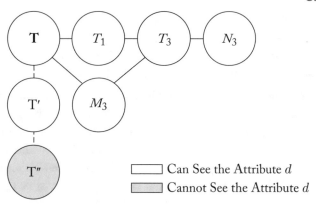

Figure C.3: Attribute visibility when T_1's privacy setting is "friends-of-friends" and T_3 has both mutual friend M_3 and non-mutual friend N_3.

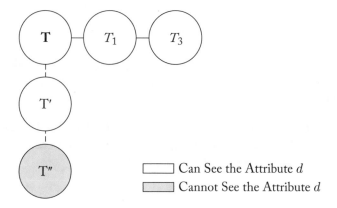

Figure C.4: Attribute visibility when T_1's privacy setting is "friends-of-friends" and T_3 has no friends except T_1.

$\{A.2, A.3\}$. Figure C.2 depicts this scenario. Other conditions remaining the same, T may have a non-mutual friend who does not have a non-mutual friend. In this case, the visibility set is assigned the value $\{A.1, A.2, A.3\}$. In addition, other conditions remaining the same, the non-mutual friend of T may have a non-mutual friend In this case also, the visibility set is assigned the value $\{A.1, A.2, A.3\}$.

3.1.c. Both Mutual and Non-Mutual Friends. There are mutual friend(s) between T_3 and T other than T_1, T_3 has non-mutual friend(s), T does not have a non-mutual friend In this case, the attribute is visible to the risk sources $A.1$, $A.2$, and $A.3$ (i.e., to the non-mutual friends of T_3 who are strangers with respect to T, to T's friends including mutual friends with T_3 and T_3 itself) from T's perspective and so Vis is assigned the value $\{A.1, A.2, A.3\}$. Figure C.3 depicts this scenario. Other conditions remaining the same, T may have a non-mutual friend which does not have a non-mutual friend or T may have a non-mutual friend which has a non-mutual friend. In both cases, Vis is assigned the value $\{A.1, A.2, A.3\}$.

3.1.d. Neither Mutual nor Non-Mutual Friends. There is no mutual friend between T_3 and T except T_1 and no non-mutual friend, T does not have a non-mutual friend. In other words, T_3 has no friend other than T_1. In this case, the attribute is visible to the risk source $A.2$ (i.e., to T_3 itself) from T's perspective and so Vis is assigned the value $\{A.2\}$. Figure C.4 depicts this scenario. Attribute d is visible to some friends of friends of T like T_3. This means that the attribute is visible to the risk source $A.2$, comprising some friends of friends of T. Other conditions remaining the same, T may have a non-mutual friend who does not have a non-mutual friend or T may have a non-mutual friend who has a non-mutual friend In these cases, the visibility set is assigned the values $\{A.1, A.2\}$ and $\{A.1, A.2, A.3\}$, respectively.

Scenario 2: Private Friendlist. If the friendlist of the non-mutual friend T_3 of T_1 is private or cannot be collected, then the set Vis assumes the worst-case value $\{A.1, A.2, A.3\}$. Ultimately, the visibility values obtained from checking the friendlists of the non-mutual friends T_3 of T_1 is merged with the ones obtained earlier by checking the friendlist of T_1 and assigned to $\mathbb{M}[T_1, d]$.

Case 4. An attribute d of a friend T_1 is visible from T, T', and T''. In this case, the privacy setting used by T_1 for d is "public" and, hence, the corresponding cell in the visibility matrix $\mathbb{M}[T_1, d]$ is assigned the set $\{A.1, A.2, A.3\}$.

Bibliography

[1] ILOG CPLEX. https://www-01.ibm.com/software/commerce/optimization/cplex-optimizer/index.html

[2] Younes Abid, Abdessamad Imine, Amedeo Napoli, Chedy Raïssi, and Michaël Rusinowitch. Online link disclosure strategies for social networks. In *International Conference on Risks and Security of Internet and Systems*, pages 153–168, Springer, 2016. DOI: 10.1007/978-3-319-54876-0_13 30

[3] Alessandro Acquisti and Christina Fong. An experiment in hiring discrimination via online social networks. *Management Science*, 66(3):1005–1024, 2020. DOI: 10.1287/mnsc.2018.3269 13

[4] Paul S. Adler and Seok-Woo Kwon. Social capital: Prospects for a new concept. *Academy of Management Review*, 27(1):17–40, 2002. DOI: 10.5465/amr.2002.5922314 50

[5] Erfan Aghasian, Saurabh Garg, Longxiang Gao, Shui Yu, and James Montgomery. Scoring users' privacy disclosure across multiple online social networks. *IEEE Access*, 5:13118–13130, 2017. DOI: 10.1109/access.2017.2720187 17, 18, 19, 21, 67, 73, 74

[6] Cuneyt Akcora, Barbara Carminati, and Elena Ferrari. Privacy in social networks: How risky is your social graph? In *Data Engineering (ICDE), IEEE 28th International Conference on*, pages 9–19, 2012. DOI: 10.1109/icde.2012.99 17, 22

[7] Faiyaz Al Zamal, Wendy Liu, and Derek Ruths. Homophily and latent attribute inference: Inferring latent attributes of twitter users from neighbors. *6th International AAAI Conference on Weblogs and Social Media (ICWSM)*, 270, 2012. 1, 11

[8] J. Alemany, E. del Val, J. Alberola, and Ana García-Fornes. Estimation of privacy risk through centrality metrics. *Future Generation Computer Systems*, 82:63–76, 2018. DOI: 10.1016/j.future.2017.12.030 17, 18, 19, 21, 22, 73, 74

[9] Jose Alemany, Elena Del Val, Juan M. Alberola, and Ana García-Fornes. Metrics for privacy assessment when sharing information in online social networks. *IEEE Access*, 7:143631–143645, 2019. DOI: 10.1109/access.2019.2944723 17, 19, 21, 22, 73, 74

[10] Bizhan Alipour, Abdessamad Imine, and Michaël Rusinowitch. Gender inference for Facebook picture owners. In *International Conference on Trust and Privacy in Digital Business*, pages 145–160, Springer, 2019. DOI: 10.1007/978-3-030-27813-7_10 10, 11

[11] Athanasios Andreou, Giridhari Venkatadri, Oana Goga, Krishna P. Gummadi, Patrick Loiseau, and Alan Mislove. Investigating ad transparency mechanisms in social media: A case study of Facebook explanations. In *25th Annual Network and Distributed System Security Symposium, (NDSS)*, San Diego, CA, February 18–21, 2018. DOI: 10.14722/ndss.2018.23191 5, 8

[12] John A. Bargh and Katelyn YA McKenna. The Internet and social life. *Annual Review of Psychology*, 55:573–590, 2004. DOI: 10.1146/annurev.psych.55.090902.141922 50, 52

[13] John A. Bargh, Katelyn YA McKenna, and Grainne M. Fitzsimons. Can you see the real me? Activation and expression of the "true self" on the Internet. *Journal of Social Issues*, 58(1):33–48, 2002. DOI: 10.1111/1540-4560.00247 52

[14] BBC News. Facebook's data-sharing deals exposed, 2018. https://www.bbc.com/news/technology-46618582 5

[15] Justin Becker and Hao Chen. Measuring privacy risk in online social networks. In *Proc. of the Workshop on Web*, 2, 2009. 17, 18, 19, 20, 22, 73, 74

[16] Gergely Biczók and Pern Hui Chia. Interdependent privacy: Let me share your data. In *International Conference on Financial Cryptography and Data Security*, pages 338–353, Springer, 2013. DOI: 10.1007/978-3-642-39884-1_29 60, 61

[17] Igor Bilogrevic, Kévin Huguenin, Berker Agir, Murtuza Jadliwala, Maria Gazaki, and Jean-Pierre Hubaux. A machine-learning based approach to privacy-aware information-sharing in mobile social networks. *Pervasive and Mobile Computing*, 25:125–142, 2016. DOI: 10.1016/j.pmcj.2015.01.006 60

[18] Igor Bilogrevic, Kévin Huguenin, Berker Agir, Murtuza Jadliwala, and Jean-Pierre Hubaux. Adaptive information-sharing for privacy-aware mobile social networks. In *Proc. of the ACM International Joint Conference on Pervasive and Ubiquitous Computing*, pages 657–666, 2013. DOI: 10.1145/2493432.2493510 60

[19] Julia Borghoff, Lars R. Knudsen, and Mathias Stolpe. Bivium as a mixed-integer linear programming problem. In *IMA International Conference*, pages 133–152, Springer, 2009. DOI: 10.1007/978-3-642-10868-6_9 62

[20] Pierre Bourdieu and Loïc J. D. Wacquant. *An Invitation to Reflexive Sociology*. University of Chicago Press, 1992. 50

[21] Petter Bae Brandtzæg, Marika Lüders, and Jan Håvard Skjetne. Too many Facebook "friends"? Content sharing and sociability versus the need for privacy in social network sites. *International Journal of Human–Computer Interaction*, 26(11–12):1006–1030, 2010. DOI: 10.1080/10447318.2010.516719 14

[22] Moira Burke, Robert Kraut, and Cameron Marlow. Social capital on Facebook: Differentiating uses and users. In *Proc. of the SIGCHI Conference on Human Factors in Computing Systems*, pages 571–580, 2011. DOI: 10.1145/1978942.1979023 49

[23] Moira Burke, Cameron Marlow, and Thomas Lento. Social network activity and social well-being. In *Proc. of the SIGCHI Conference on Human Factors in Computing Systems*, pages 1909–1912, 2010. DOI: 10.1145/1753326.1753613 49

[24] Ryan Calo. The boundaries of privacy harm. *Indiana Law Journal*, 86:1131–1617, 2011. 12

[25] Ryan Calo. Privacy harm exceptionalism. *Colorado Technology Law Journal*, 12:361–364, 2014. 12

[26] A Risk-based approach to privacy: Improving effectiveness in practice, Centre for Information Policy Leadership (CIPL) Hunton & Williams LLP, 2014. https://www.informationpolicycentre.com/uploads/5/7/1/0/57104281/white_paper_1-a_risk_based_approach_to_privacy_improving_effectiveness_in_practice.pdf 15

[27] Abdelberi Chaabane, Gergely Acs, Mohamed Ali Kaafar, et al. You are what you like! information leakage through users' interests. In *Proc. of the 19th Annual Network and Distributed System Security Symposium (NDSS)*, 2012. 10, 11

[28] Jundong Chen, Matthias R. Brust, Ankunda R. Kiremire, and Vir V. Phoha. Modeling privacy settings of an online social network from a game-theoretical perspective. In *9th International Conference Conference on Collaborative Computing: Networking, Applications and Worksharing*, pages 213–220, IEEE, 2013. DOI: 10.4108/icst.collaboratecom.2013.254054 60, 61

[29] Jundong Chen, Ankunda R. Kiremire, Matthias R. Brust, and Vir V. Phoha. A game theoretic approach for modeling privacy settings of an online social network. *EAI Endorsed Transactions on Collaborative Computing*, 1(1):e4, 2014. DOI: 10.4108/cc.1.1.e4 60, 61

[30] Roger Clarke. Privacy impact assessments, 1999. http://www.xamax.com.au/DV/PIA.html 15

[31] Julie E. Cohen. Examined lives: Informational privacy and the subject as object. *Stanford Law Review*, pages 1373–1438, 2000. DOI: 10.2307/1229517 12

[32] Commission Nationale de l'Informatique et des Libertes (CNIL). Privacy Impact Assessment (PIA) 1: Methodology, 2018. https://www.cnil.fr/sites/default/files/atoms/files/cnil-pia-1-en-methodology.pdf 14, 15

[33] Commission Nationale de l'Informatique et des Libertes (CNIL). Privacy Impact Assessment (PIA) 2: Template, 2018. https://www.cnil.fr/sites/default/files/atoms/files/cnil-pia-2-en-templates.pdf 15

[34] Commission Nationale de l'Informatique et des Libertes (CNIL). Privacy Impact Assessment (PIA) 3: Knowledge Bases, 2018. https://www.cnil.fr/sites/default/files/atoms/files/cnil-pia-3-en-knowldedgebases.pdf 14, 15, 46

[35] Kate Crawford and Jason Schultz. Big data and due process: Toward a framework to redress predictive privacy harms. *Boston College Law Review*, 55:93–130, 2014. 12

[36] Gabriel J. X. Dance, Michael La Forgia, and Nicholas Confessore. As Facebook raised a privacy wall, it carved an opening for tech giants, 2018. https://www.nytimes.com/2018/12/18/technology/facebook-privacy.html 5

[37] Amit Datta, Anupam Datta, Jael Makagon, Deirdre K. Mulligan, and Michael Carl Tschantz. Discrimination in online advertising: A multidisciplinary inquiry. In *Proc. of the 1st Conference on Fairness, Accountability and Transparency, (PMLR)*, 81, 2018. 8

[38] Sourya Joyee De and Abdessamad Imine. Consent for targeted advertising: The case of Facebook. *AI and Society*. DOI: 10.1007/s00146-020-00981-5 5

[39] Sourya Joyee De and Abdessamad Imine. Privacy scoring of social network user profiles through risk analysis. In *12th International Conference on Risks and Security of Internet and Systems*, Springer, 2017. DOI: 10.1007/978-3-319-76687-4_16 2, 5, 10, 11, 12, 13, 15, 17, 18, 19, 20, 21, 22, 23, 31, 34, 37, 73, 74

[40] Sourya Joyee De and Abdessamad Imine. Enabling users to balance social benefit and privacy in online social networks. In *Proc. of 16th Annual Conference on Privacy Security and Trust (PST)*, IEEE, 2018. DOI: 10.1109/pst.2018.8514202 2, 11, 12, 15, 19, 20, 22, 31, 49, 51, 55, 60, 62, 64

[41] Sourya Joyee De and Abdessamad Imine. On consent in online social networks: Privacy impacts and research directions (short paper). In *Proc. of 13th International Conference on Risks and Security of Internet and Systems*, Springer, 2018. DOI: 10.1007/978-3-030-12143-3_11 2, 12, 19, 20, 22, 33

[42] Sourya Joyee De and Abdessamad Imine. To reveal or not to reveal—balancing user-centric social benefit and privacy in online social networks. In *Proc. of the 33rd Annual ACM Symposium on Applied Computing (ACM SAC)*, ACM, 2018. DOI: 10.1145/3167132.3167258 11, 15, 31, 60, 61

[43] Sourya Joyee De and Daniel Le Métayer. PRIAM: A privacy risk analysis methodology. In *11th International Workshop on Data Privacy Management*, IEEE, 2016. DOI: 10.1007/978-3-319-47072-6_15 5, 8, 11, 12, 13, 14, 15, 20, 31

[44] Sourya Joyee De and Daniel Le Métayer. Privacy harm analysis: A case study on smart grids. In *International Workshop on Privacy Engineering (IWPE)*, IEEE, 2016. DOI: 10.1109/spw.2016.21 11, 12, 31

[45] Sourya Joyee De and Daniel Le Métayer. *Privacy Risk Analysis*. In Synthesis Series, Morgan & Claypool Publishers, 2016. DOI: 10.2200/s00724ed1v01y201607spt017 8, 11, 12, 13, 15, 20, 31, 32, 37

[46] Sourya Joyee De and Daniel Le Métayer. Privacy risk analysis to enable informed privacy settings. In *IEEE European Symposium on Security and Privacy Workshops (EuroS&PW)*, pages 95–102, 2018. DOI: 10.1109/eurospw.2018.00019 2, 15

[47] Sourya Joyee De and Daniel Le Métayer. A risk-based approach to privacy by design (extended version). *Number RR-9001*, December, 2016. 8, 12, 31

[48] Mina Deng, Kim Wuyts, Riccardo Scandariato, Bart Preneel, and Wouter Joosen. LINDDUN: running example-social network 2.0, 2008. https://7e71aeba-b883-4889-aee9-a3064f8be401.filesusr.com/ugd/cc602e_4e132b016cdb4822b98b4459e3c3ce76.pdf 15

[49] Mina Deng, Kim Wuyts, Riccardo Scandariato, Bart Preneel, and Wouter Joosen. A privacy threat analysis framework: Supporting the elicitation and fulfilment of privacy requirements. *Requirements Engineering*, 16(1):3–32, 2011. DOI: 10.1007/s00766-010-0115-7 15, 31

[50] Ratan Dey, Cong Tang, Keith Ross, and Nitesh Saxena. Estimating age privacy leakage in online social networks. In *INFOCOM, Proceedings IEEE*, pages 2836–2840, 2012. DOI: 10.1109/infcom.2012.6195711 10, 11

[51] Judith Donath and Danah Boyd. Public displays of connection. *BT Technology Journal*, 22(4):71–82, 2004. DOI: 10.1023/b:bttj.0000047585.06264.cc 52

[52] Nicole Ellison, Rebecca Heino, and Jennifer Gibbs. Managing impressions online: Self-presentation processes in the online dating environment. *Journal of Computer-Mediated Communication*, 11(2):415–441, 2006. DOI: 10.1111/j.1083-6101.2006.00020.x 51

[53] Nicole B. Ellison, Charles Steinfield, and Cliff Lampe. The benefits of Facebook "friends": Social capital and college students? Use of online social network sites. *Journal of Computer-Mediated Communication*, 12(4):1143–1168, 2007. DOI: 10.1111/j.1083-6101.2007.00367.x 49, 50, 51, 52, 53, 54

[54] Nicole B. Ellison, Charles Steinfield, and Cliff Lampe. Connection strategies: Social capital implications of Facebook-enabled communication practices. *New Media and Society*, 13(6):873–892, 2011. DOI: 10.1177/1461444810385389 49, 50

[55] Nicole B. Ellison, Jessica Vitak, Rebecca Gray, and Cliff Lampe. Cultivating social resources on social network sites: Facebook relationship maintenance behaviors and their role in social capital processes. *Journal of Computer-Mediated Communication*, 19(4):855–870, 2014. DOI: 10.1111/jcc4.12078 49, 50, 52

[56] European Commission. General Data Protection Regulation, 2016. https://eur-lex.europa.eu/legal-content/EN/TXT/PDF/?uri=CELEX:32016R0679 2, 6, 15, 21, 37, 59

[57] Tara Evans. Sharp rise in identity fraud, 2016. http://www.telegraph.co.uk/money/consumer-affairs/sharp-rise-in-identity-fraud-as-scammers-use-facebook-and-other/ 13

[58] Expert Group 2 of Smart Grid Task Force. Data Protection Impact Assessment Template for Smart Grid and Smart Metering Systems, 2014. https://ec.europa.eu/energy/sites/ener/files/documents/dpia_for_publication_2018.pdf 15

[59] Jesús Friginal, Jérémie Guiochet, and Marc-Olivier Killijian. Towards a privacy risk assessment methodology for location-based systems. In *Mobile and Ubiquitous Systems: Computing, Networking, and Services*, pages 748–753, Springer, 2014. DOI: 10.1007/978-3-319-11569-6_65 15, 31

[60] Michael Garcia, Naomi Lefkovitz, and Suzanne Lightman. *Privacy Risk Management for Federal Information Systems (NISTIR 8062 (Draft))*. National Institute of Standards and Technology, 2015. 15

[61] Jennifer L. Gibbs, Nicole B. Ellison, and Rebecca D. Heino. Self-presentation in online personals: The role of anticipated future interaction, self-disclosure, and perceived success in Internet dating. *Communication Research*, 33(2):152–177, 2006. DOI: 10.1177/0093650205285368 51, 52, 53

[62] Neil Zhenqiang Gong and Bin Liu. You are who you know and how you behave: Attribute inference attacks via users' social friends and behaviors. In *USENIX Security Symposium*, pages 979–995, 2016. 8, 10, 11

[63] Neil Zhenqiang Gong and Bin Liu. Attribute inference attacks in online social networks. *ACM Transactions on Privacy and Security (TOPS)*, 21(1):1–30, 2018. DOI: 10.1145/3154793 8, 10

[64] Neil Zhenqiang Gong, Ameet Talwalkar, Lester Mackey, Ling Huang, Eui Chul Richard Shin, Emil Stefanov, Elaine Shi, and Dawn Song. Joint link prediction and attribute inference using a social-attribute network. *ACM Transactions on Intelligent Systems and Technology (TIST)*, 5(2):1–20, 2014. DOI: 10.1145/2594455 10, 11

[65] John Gramlich.   10 Facts About Americans and Facebook, 2019.   https://www.
pewresearch.org/fact-tank/2019/05/16/facts-about-americans-and-facebook/ 1, 5

[66] Mark Granovetter. The strength of weak ties: A network theory revisited. *Sociological Theory*, pages 201–233, 1983. DOI: 10.2307/202051 49

[67] Mark S. Granovetter. The strength of weak ties. *American Journal of Sociology*, 78(6):1360–1380, 1973. DOI: 10.1086/225469 50

[68] Ralph Gross and Alessandro Acquisti. Information revelation and privacy in online social networks. In *ACM Workshop on Privacy in the Electronic Society*, pages 71–80, 2005. DOI: 10.1145/1102199.1102214 5, 13

[69] Shumin Guo and Keke Chen. Mining privacy settings to find optimal privacy-utility tradeoffs for social network services. In *International Conference on Privacy, Security, Risk and Trust and International Conference on Social Computing*, pages 656–665, IEEE, 2012. DOI: 10.1109/socialcom-passat.2012.22 60, 61

[70] Caroline Haythornthwaite. Strong, weak, and latent ties and the impact of new media. *The Information Society*, 18(5):385–401, 2002. DOI: 10.1080/01972240290108195 49

[71] Caroline Haythornthwaite. Social networks and internet connectivity effects. *Information, Community and Society*, 8(2):125–147, 2005. DOI: 10.1080/13691180500146185 49, 53

[72] Jianming He, Wesley W. Chu, and Zhenyu Victor Liu. Inferring privacy information from social networks. In *International Conference on Intelligence and Security Informatics*, pages 154–165, Springer, 2006. DOI: 10.1007/11760146_14 10

[73] John F. Helliwell and Robert D. Putnam. The social context of well-being. *Philosophical Transactions of the Royal Society of London. Series B: Biological Sciences*, 359(1449):1435–1446, 2004. DOI: 10.1098/rstb.2004.1522 50

[74] S. Hillier Frederick and J. Lieberman Gerald. *Introduction to Operations Research*, McGraw-Hill, 2005. 62

[75] Lei Huang and Dan Wang. What a surprise: Initial connection with coworkers on Facebook and expectancy violations. In *19th ACM Conference on Computer Supported Cooperative Work and Social Computing Companion*, pages 293–296, 2016. DOI: 10.1145/2818052.2869081 5, 12, 13, 52, 53

[76] IBM. Using CPLEX to examine alternate optimal solutions. http://www-01.ibm.com/support/docview.wss?uid=swg21399929 62

[77] Faizullabhoy Irfan and Korolova Aleksandra. Facebook's advertising platform: New attack vectors and the need for interventions. *CoRR*, 2018. 5, 8

[78] Jinyuan Jia, Binghui Wang, Le Zhang, and Neil Zhenqiang Gong. Attriinfer: Inferring user attributes in online social networks using markov random fields. In *Proc. of the 26th International Conference on World Wide Web*, pages 1561–1569, 2017. DOI: 10.1145/3038912.3052695 10, 11

[79] Maritza Johnson, Serge Egelman, and Steven M. Bellovin. Facebook and privacy: It's complicated. In *8th Symposium on Usable Privacy and Security*, 9, ACM, 2012. DOI: 10.1145/2335356.2335369 5, 13

[80] Adam N. Joinson. Looking at, looking up or keeping up with people? Motives and use of Facebook. In *Proc. of the SIGCHI Conference on Human Factors in Computing Systems*, pages 1027–1036, 2008. DOI: 10.1145/1357054.1357213 52

[81] Charles A. Kamhoua, Kevin A. Kwiat, and Joon S. Park. A game theoretic approach for modeling optimal data sharing on online social networks. In *2012 9th International Conference on Electrical Engineering, Computing Science and Automatic Control (CCE)*, pages 1–6, IEEE, 2012. DOI: 10.1109/iceee.2012.6421108 60, 61

[82] M.H.R. Khouzani, Pasquale Malacaria, Chris Hankin, Andrew Fielder, and Fabrizio Smeraldi. Efficient numerical frameworks for multi-objective cyber security planning. In *European Symposium on Research in Computer Security*, pages 179–197, Springer, 2016. DOI: 10.1007/978-3-319-45741-3_10 62

[83] Barbara Kordy, Piotr Kordy, Sjouke Mauw, and Patrick Schweitzer. ADTool: Security analysis with attack-defense trees. In *Quantitative Evaluation of Systems*, pages 173–176, Springer, 2013. DOI: 10.1007/978-3-642-40196-1_15 31

[84] Barbara Kordy, Sjouke Mauw, Saša Radomirović, and Patrick Schweitzer. Attack-defense trees. *Journal of Logic and Computation*, exs029, 2012. DOI: 10.1093/logcom/exs029 31

[85] Aleksandra Korolova. Privacy violations using microtargeted ads: A case study. In *The 10th IEEE International Conference on Data Mining Workshops (ICDMW)*, pages 474–482, Sydney, Australia, December 13, 2010. DOI: 10.1109/ICDMW.2010.137 5

[86] Michal Kosinski, David Stillwell, and Thore Graepel. Private traits and attributes are predictable from digital records of human behavior. *Proc. of the National Academy of Sciences*, 110(15):5802–5805, 2013. DOI: 10.1073/pnas.1218772110 10

[87] Hanna Krasnova, Oliver Günther, Sarah Spiekermann, and Ksenia Koroleva. Privacy concerns and identity in online social networks. *Identity in the Information Society*, 2(1):39–63, 2009. DOI: 10.1007/s12394-009-0019-1 59, 63

[88] Hanna Krasnova, Sarah Spiekermann, Ksenia Koroleva, and Thomas Hildebrand. Online social networks: Why we disclose. *Journal of Information Technology*, 25(2):109–125, 2010. DOI: 10.1057/jit.2010.6 1, 51, 52, 53

[89] Sebastian Labitzke, Florian Werling, Jens Mittag, and Hannes Hartenstein. Do online social network friends still threaten my privacy? In *Proc. of the 3rd ACM Conference on Data and Application Security and Privacy*, pages 13–24, 2013. DOI: 10.1145/2435349.2435352 10

[90] Cliff A. C. Lampe, Nicole Ellison, and Charles Steinfield. A familiar face (book): Profile elements as signals in an online social network. In *SIGCHI Conference on Human Factors in Computing Systems*, pages 435–444, ACM, 2007. DOI: 10.1145/1240624.1240695 52, 53, 54

[91] Dave Lee. Facebook security breach: Up to 50 m accounts attacked, 2018. https://www.bbc.com/news/technology-45686890 5

[92] Dave Lee. Facebook sued by top prosecutor over Cambridge Analytica, 2018. https://www.bbc.com/news/technology-46627133 5

[93] Amanda Lenhart. Adults and social network websites. *Pew Internet & American Life Project*, 2009. 52

[94] Nan Lin. *Social Capital: A Theory of Social Structure and Action*, vol. 19. Cambridge University Press, 2002. DOI: 10.1017/cbo9780511815447 50

[95] Kun Liu and Evimaria Terzi. A Framework for computing the privacy scores of users in online social networks. *ACM Transactions on Knowledge Discovery from Data*, 5(1):6, 2010. DOI: 10.1145/1870096.1870102 17, 18, 19, 20, 21, 73, 74

[96] Wendy Liu and Derek Ruths. What's in a name? Using first names as features for gender inference in twitter. In *AAAI Spring Symposium Series*, 2013. 11

[97] Miller McPherson, Lynn Smith-Lovin, and James M. Cook. Birds of a feather: Homophily in social networks. *Annual Review of Sociology*, 27(1):415–444, 2001. DOI: 10.1146/annurev.soc.27.1.415 1, 10

[98] Alan Mislove, Sune Lehmann, Yong-Yeol Ahn, Jukka-Pekka Onnela, and J. Niels Rosenquist. Understanding the demographics of Twitter users. In *5th International AAAI Conference on Weblogs and Social Media*, 2011. 11

[99] Alan Mislove, Bimal Viswanath, Krishna P. Gummadi, and Peter Druschel. You are who you know: Inferring user profiles in online social networks. In *Proc. of the 3rd ACM International Conference on Web Search and Data Mining*, pages 251–260, 2010. DOI: 10.1145/1718487.1718519 1, 10

[100] Juergen Mueller and Gerd Stumme. Gender inference using statistical name characteristics in twitter. In *Proc. of the 3rd Multidisciplinary International Social Networks Conference on Social Informatics, Data Science*, pages 1–8, 2016. DOI: 10.1145/2955129.2955182 11

[101] Roger B. Myerson. *Game Theory: Analysis of Conflict*, Harvard University Press, 2013. DOI: 10.2307/j.ctvjsf522 61

[102] Miguel Nunez del Prado Cortez and Jesús Friginal. Geo-location inference attacks: From modelling to privacy risk assessment. In *10th European Dependable Computing Conference (EDCC)*, pages 222–225, IEEE, 2014. DOI: 10.1109/edcc.2014.32 31

[103] Dierdre O'Brien and Ann M. Torres. Social networking and online privacy: Facebook users' perceptions. *Irish Journal of Management*, 2012. 13, 59, 63

[104] Marie Caroline Oetzel and Sarah Spiekermann. A systematic methodology for privacy impact assessments: A design science approach. *European Journal of Information Systems*, 23(2):126–150, 2014. DOI: 10.1057/ejis.2013.18 15

[105] Marie Caroline Oetzel, Sarah Spiekermann, Ingrid Grüning, Harald Kelter, and Sabine Mull. Privacy impact assessment guideline for RFID applications, *Federal Office for Information Security (BSI), Germany*, 2011. 15

[106] Paul Ohm. Broken promises of privacy: Responding to the surprising failure of anonymization. *UCLA Law Review*, 57:1701–1819, 2010. 12

[107] Paul Ohm. Sensitive information. *Southern California Law Review*, 88:1125–1180, 2015. 12

[108] Ariane Ollier-Malaterre, Nancy P. Rothbard, and Justin M. Berg. When worlds collide in cyberspace: How boundary work in online social networks impacts professional relationships. *Academy of Management Review*, 38(4):645–669, 2013. DOI: 10.5465/amr.2011.0235 5, 12, 13

[109] A.-M. Olteanu, Mathias Humbert, Kévin Huguenin, and J.-P. Hubaux. The (co)location sharing game: Benefits and privacy implications of (co)-location sharing with interdependences. *Proc. on Privacy Enhancing Technologies*, 2, 2019. 60, 61

[110] Alexandra Mihaela Olteanu, Kévin Huguenin, Mathias Humbert, and Jean-Pierre Hubaux. The sharing game: Benefits and privacy implications of (co)-location sharing with interdependences. *Technical Report*, 2016. 60, 61

[111] Martin J. Osborne and Ariel Rubinstein. *A Course in Game Theory*. MIT Press, 1994. 61

[112] Samia Oukemeni, Helena Rifà-Pous, and Joan Manuel Marquès Puig. IPAM: Information privacy assessment metric in microblogging online social networks. *IEEE Access*, 7:114817–114836, 2019. DOI: 10.1109/access.2019.2932899 17

[113] Joon S. Park, Kevin A. Kwiat, Charles A. Kamhoua, Jonathan White, and Sookyung Kim. Trusted online social network (OSN) services with optimal data management. *Computers and Security*, 42:116–136, 2014. DOI: 10.1016/j.cose.2014.02.004 60, 61

[114] Tiffany A. Pempek, Yevdokiya A. Yermolayeva, and Sandra L. Calvert. College students' social networking experiences on Facebook. *Journal of Applied Developmental Psychology*, 30(3):227–238, 2009. DOI: 10.1016/j.appdev.2008.12.010 52, 54

[115] Thierry Pénard and Nicolas Poussing. Internet use and social capital: The strength of virtual ties. *Journal of Economic Issues*, 44(3):569–595, 2010. DOI: 10.2753/JEI0021-3624440301 50

[116] David Pergament, Armen Aghasaryan, Jean-Gabriel Ganascia, and Stéphane Betgé-Brezetz. FORPS: Friends-oriented reputation privacy score. In *Proc. of the 1st International Workshop on Security and Privacy Preserving in e-Societies*, pages 19–25, ACM, 2011. DOI: 10.1145/2107581.2107585 17, 20, 22

[117] Georgios Petkos, Symeon Papadopoulos, and Yiannis Kompatsiaris. PScore: A framework for enhancing privacy awareness in online social networks. In *Availability, Reliability and Security (ARES), 10th International Conference on*, pages 592–600, IEEE, 2015. DOI: 10.1109/ares.2015.80 17, 18, 20, 21, 22, 73, 74

[118] Bizhan Alipour Pijani, Abdessamad Imine, and Michaël Rusinowitch. You are what emojis say about your pictures: Language-independent gender inference attack on Facebook. In *Proc. of the 35th Annual ACM Symposium on Applied Computing*, pages 1826–1834, 2020. DOI: 10.1145/3341105.3373943 10, 11

[119] Robert D. Putnam et al. *Bowling Alone: The Collapse and Revival of American Community*. Simon and Schuster, 2000. DOI: 10.1145/358916.361990 50

[120] Yasmin Rafiq, Luke Dickens, Alessandra Russo, Arosha K. Bandara, Mu Yang, Avelie Stuart, Mark Levine, Gul Calikli, Blaine A. Price, and Bashar Nuseibeh. Learning to share: Engineering adaptive decision-support for online social networks. In *32nd IEEE/ACM International Conference on Automated Software Engineering (ASE)*, pages 280–285, 2017. DOI: 10.1109/ase.2017.8115641 60, 61

[121] Yasmin Rafiq, Luke Dickens, Mu Yang, Alessandra Russo, Radu Calinescu, Arosha K. Bandara, Blaine A. Price, Avelie Stuart, Mark Levine, and Bashar Nuseibeh. Learning to share: Using probabilistic models for adaptive sharing in online social networks. In *11th International Symposium on Software Engineering for Adaptive and Self-Managing Systems (submitted for review), SEAMS*, 16, 2016. 60, 61

[122] Filipe N. Ribeiro, Koustuv Saha, Mahmoudreza Babaei, Lucas Henrique, Johnnatan Messias, Fabricio Benevenuto, Oana Goga, Krishna P. Gummadi, and Elissa M. Redmiles. On microtargeting socially divisive ads: A case study of russia-linked ad campaigns on Facebook. In *Proc. of the Conference on Fairness, Accountability, and Transparency*, pages 140–149, ACM, 2019. DOI: 10.1145/3287560.3287580 5, 8

[123] Michelle Richey, Aparna Gonibeed, and M. N. Ravishankar. The perils and promises of self-disclosure on social media. *Information Systems Frontiers*, 20(3):425–437, 2018. DOI: 10.1007/s10796-017-9806-7 13

[124] Arpan Roy, Dong Seong Kim, and Kishor S. Trivedi. Attack countermeasure trees (act): Towards unifying the constructs of attack and defense trees. *Security and Communication Networks*, 5(8):929–943, 2012. DOI: 10.1002/sec.299 31

[125] Bruce Schneier. Attack trees. *Dr. Dobb's Journal*, 24(12):21–29, 1999. DOI: 10.1002/9781119183631.ch21 31

[126] Smith, Aaron. Why americans use social media, 2011. https://www.pewresearch.org/internet/2011/11/15/why-americans-use-social-media/ 1

[127] Andrew D. Smock, Nicole B. Ellison, Cliff Lampe, and Donghee Yvette Wohn. Facebook as a toolkit: A uses and gratification approach to unbundling feature use. *Computers in Human Behavior*, 27(6):2322–2329, 2011. DOI: 10.1016/j.chb.2011.07.011 52

[128] Daniel J. Solove. A taxonomy of privacy. *University of Pennsylvania Law Review*, pages 477–564, 2006. DOI: 10.2307/40041279 12

[129] Till Speicher, Muhammad Ali, Giridhari Venkatadri, Filipe Nunes Ribeiro, George Arvanitakis, Fabrício Benevenuto, Krishna P. Gummadi, Patrick Loiseau, and Alan Mislove. Potential for discrimination in online targeted advertising. In *Conference on Fairness, Accountability and Transparency, (FAT)*, pages 5–19, New York, February 23–24, 2018. 5, 8

[130] Anna Cinzia Squicciarini and Christopher Griffin. An informed model of personal information release in social networking sites. In *International Conference on Privacy, Security, Risk and Trust (PASSAT) and International Confernece on Social Computing (SocialCom)*, pages 636–645, IEEE, 2012. DOI: 10.1109/socialcom-passat.2012.137 60, 61

[131] Anna Cinzia Squicciarini, Mohamed Shehab, and Federica Paci. Collective privacy management in social networks. In *Proc. of the 18th International Conference on World Wide Web*, pages 521–530, ACM, 2009. DOI: 10.1145/1526709.1526780 60, 61

[132] Agrima Srivastava and G. Geethakumari. Measuring privacy leaks in online social networks. In *Advances in Computing, Communications and Informatics (ICACCI), International Conference on*, pages 2095–2100, IEEE, 2013. DOI: 10.1109/icacci.2013.6637504 17

[133] Statista. Penetration rate of leading social networks in France during the third quarter of 2019, 2019. https://www.statista.com/statistics/284435/social-network-penetration-france/ 1

[134] Statista. Leading Countries based on Facebook Audience Size as of April 2020, 2020. https://www.statista.com/statistics/268136/top-15-countries-based-on-number-of-facebook-users/ 1, 5

[135] Charles Steinfield, Nicole B. Ellison, and Cliff Lampe. Social capital, self-esteem, and use of online social network sites: A longitudinal analysis. *Journal of Applied Developmental Psychology*, 29(6):434–445, 2008. DOI: 10.1016/j.appdev.2008.07.002 49

[136] Kaveri Subrahmanyam, Stephanie M. Reich, Natalia Waechter, and Guadalupe Espinoza. Online and offline social networks: Use of social networking sites by emerging adults. *Journal of Applied Developmental Psychology*, 29(6):420–433, 2008. DOI: 10.1016/j.appdev.2008.07.003 52

[137] Nilothpal Talukder, Mourad Ouzzani, Ahmed K. Elmagarmid, Hazem Elmeleegy, and Mohamed Yakout. Privometer: Privacy protection in social networks. In *Data Engineering Workshops (ICDEW), IEEE 26th International Conference on*, pages 266–269, 2010. DOI: 10.1109/icdew.2010.5452715 17, 18, 19, 20, 73, 74

[138] Cong Tang, Keith Ross, Nitesh Saxena, and Ruichuan Chen. What's in a name: A study of names, gender inference, and gender behavior in Facebook. In *International Conference on Database Systems for Advanced Applications*, pages 344–356, Springer, 2011. DOI: 10.1007/978-3-642-20244-5_33 11

[139] Mike Thelwall and David Wilkinson. Public dialogs in social network sites: What is their purpose? *Journal of the American Society for Information Science and Technology*, 61(2):392–404, 2010. DOI: 10.1002/asi.21241 52

[140] Kurt Thomas, Chris Grier, and David M. Nicol. Unfriendly: Multi-party privacy risks in social networks. In *International Symposium on Privacy Enhancing Technologies Symposium*, pages 236–252, Springer, 2010. DOI: 10.1007/978-3-642-14527-8_14 10

[141] Lisa Collins Tidwell and Joseph B. Walther. Computer-mediated communication effects on disclosure, impressions, and interpersonal evaluations: Getting to know one another a bit at a time. *Human Communication Research*, 28(3):317–348, 2002. DOI: 10.1111/j.1468-2958.2002.tb00811.x 52

[142] S. Tong and Joseph B. Walther. Relational maintenance and CMC. *Computer-Mediated Communication in Personal Relationships*, 53:98–118, 2011. 52

[143] Zeynep Tufekci. Grooming, gossip, Facebook and MySpace: What can we learn about these sites from those who won't assimilate? *Information, Communication and Society*, 11(4):544–564, 2008. DOI: 10.1080/13691180801999050 52

[144] Sebastián Valenzuela, Namsu Park, and Kerk F. Kee. Is there social capital in a social network site?: Facebook use and college students' life satisfaction, trust, and participation. *Journal of Computer-Mediated Communication*, 14(4):875–901, 2009. DOI: 10.1111/j.1083-6101.2009.01474.x 49

[145] Giridhari Venkatadri, Athanasios Andreou, Yabing Liu, Alan Mislove, Krishna P. Gummadi, Patrick Loiseau, and Oana Goga. Privacy risks with Facebook's PII-based targeting: Auditing a data broker's advertising interface. In *IEEE Symposium on Security and Privacy (SP)*, pages 221–239, 2018. DOI: 10.1109/sp.2018.00014 5, 8

[146] Giridhari Venkatadri, Elena Lucherini, Piotr Sapiezynski, and Alan Mislove. Investigating sources of PII used in Facebook's targeted advertising. *Proc. on Privacy Enhancing Technologies*, 1:18, 2019. DOI: 10.2478/popets-2019-0013 5, 8

[147] B. S. Vidyalakshmi, Raymond K. Wong, and Chi-Hung Chi. Privacy scoring of social network users as a service. In *Services Computing (SCC), IEEE International Conference on*, pages 218–225, 2015. DOI: 10.1109/scc.2015.38 17, 22

[148] Qiaozhi Wang, Hao Xue, Fengjun Li, Dongwon Lee, and Bo Luo. # DontTweetThis: Scoring private information in social networks. *Proc. on Privacy Enhancing Technologies*, 2019(4):72–92, 2019. DOI: 10.2478/popets-2019-0059 17, 18, 19, 20, 22

[149] Yang Wang, Gregory Norcie, Saranga Komanduri, Alessandro Acquisti, Pedro Giovanni Leon, and Lorrie Faith Cranor. I regretted the minute I pressed share: A qualitative study of regrets on Facebook. In *7th Symposium on Usable Privacy and Security*, 10, ACM, 2011. DOI: 10.1145/2078827.2078841 5, 12, 13

[150] Yong Wang and Raj Kumar Nepali. Privacy measurement for social network actor model. In *Social Computing (SocialCom), International Conference on*, pages 659–664, IEEE, 2013. DOI: 10.1109/socialcom.2013.99 17, 20, 21, 73, 74

[151] Udi Weinsberg, Smriti Bhagat, Stratis Ioannidis, and Nina Taft. BlurMe: Inferring and obfuscating user gender based on ratings. In *Proc. of the 6th ACM Conference on Recommender Systems*, pages 195–202, 2012. DOI: 10.1145/2365952.2365989 10, 11

[152] Dmitri Williams. On and off the net: Scales for social capital in an online era. *Journal of Computer-Mediated Communication*, 11(2):593–628, 2006. DOI: 10.1111/j.1083-6101.2006.00029.x 50

[153] Robert E. Wilson, Samuel D. Gosling, and Lindsay T. Graham. A review of Facebook research in the social sciences. *Perspectives on Psychological Science*, 7(3):203–220, 2012. DOI: 10.1177/1745691612442904 52

[154] David Wright and Paul De Hert. Introduction to privacy impact assessment. In *Privacy Impact Assessment*, pages 3–32, Springer, 2012. DOI: 10.1007/978-94-007-2543-0_1 14

[155] David Wright, Rachel Finn, and Rowena Rodrigues. A comparative analysis of privacy impact assessment in six countries. *Journal of Contemporary European Research*, 9(1):2013. 15

[156] Kim Wuyts. Privacy threats in software architectures. Doctoral thesis, KU Leuven, 2014. 15, 31

[157] Ronald R. Yager. Trees and their role in security modeling using attack trees. *Information Sciences*, 176(20):2933–2959, 2006. DOI: 10.1016/j.ins.2005.08.004 31, 32, 33

[158] Mu Yang, Yijun Yu, Arosha K. Bandara, and Bashar Nuseibeh. Adaptive sharing for online social networks: A trade-off between privacy risk and social benefit. In *IEEE 13th International Conference on Trust, Security and Privacy in Computing and Communications*, pages 45–52, 2014. DOI: 10.1109/trustcom.2014.10 60

[159] Alyson L. Young and Anabel Quan-Haase. Information revelation and internet privacy concerns on social network sites: A case study of Facebook. In *Proc. of the 4th International Conference on Communities and Technologies*, pages 265–274, 2009. DOI: 10.1145/1556460.1556499 13

[160] Shanyang Zhao, Sherri Grasmuck, and Jason Martin. Identity construction on Facebook: Digital empowerment in anchored relationships. *Computers in Human Behavior*, 24(5):1816–1836, 2008. DOI: 10.1016/j.chb.2008.02.012 51

[161] Elena Zheleva and Lise Getoor. To join or not to join: The illusion of privacy in social networks with mixed public and private user profiles. In *Proc. of the 18th International Conference on World Wide Web*, pages 531–540, ACM, 2009. DOI: 10.1145/1526709.1526781 1, 10, 34, 45, 63

Authors' Biographies

SOURYA JOYEE DE

Sourya Joyee De is an Assistant Professor in IT & Systems at Indian Institute of Management Raipur, India. She is a Fellow of Indian Institute of Management Calcutta (Ph.D.). Prior to joining IIM Raipur, Sourya held research positions at INRIA Grenoble Rhone-Alpes and LORIA-CNRS-INRIA Nancy Grand-Est, France for close to four years. Her research has been funded by the French ANR project BIOPRIV, CISCO San Jose, CA, USA, Samsung GRO Grant, INRIA Project Lab CAPPRIS, and the Grand-Est Region, France. Sourya was also a Visiting Scientist at Indian Statistical Institute Kolkata, India. Her research interests include privacy risk analysis, user consent in the context of privacy, privacy policies, security in cloud computing, and rational cryptography. Her research has been published at various reputed journals and conferences. She has also published a book titled *Privacy Risk Analysis* with Morgan & Claypool Publishers, San Rafel, CA, USA.

ABDESSAMAD IMINE

Abdessamad Imine received M.Sc. and Ph.D. degrees in Computer Science from University of Sciences and Technology of Oran (USTO), Algeria, and University Henri Poincaré of Nancy, France, respectively. He is currently an Associate Professor HdR at Lorraine University and senior researcher at LORIA center of Nancy. His research interests include privacy in social networks, security for collaborative systems, optimistic protocols, and formal methods. Abdessamad Imine has developed a formal methodology for specifying and verifying the consistency of synchronized objects by operational transformation. This methodology has been successfully used in the design of a configuration management system in the LibreSource project. He has also devised protocols for controlling and enforcing privacy in social networks and protocols for synchronizing and securing shared data such as text, XML, and RDF documents. He is author and co-author of more than 82 papers in international conferences, journals, and books.

Printed in the United States
by Baker & Taylor Publisher Services